THE MOST DANGEROUS DECADE

THE MOST DANGEROUS DECADE

*World Militarism and the New
Non-aligned Peace Movement*

Ken Coates

SPOKESMAN

First published in 1984 by:
Spokesman
Bertrand Russell House
Gamble Street
Nottingham, England
Tel. 0602 708318

British Library Cataloguing in Publication Data

Coates, Ken
The most dangerous decade.
1. War
I. Title
355'.0217   U21.2
ISBN 0-85124-405-X Hardcase
ISBN 0-85124-406-8 Paperback

Contents

Introduction

As this book goes to the printers, five hundred more courageous women have joined the seige of Greenham Common. Defying arbitrary arrest, intimidation by bailiffs, and appalling weather, these women and their counterparts all over Europe have spoken for conscience and acted for common humanity in a world which seems inexorably bent upon mutual genocide.

Genocide is a crime. In order to be punished for it, hitherto, its instigators have had to lose a war. Since this happened in 1945, there have been recurrent acts which any impartial persons will regard as coming uncomfortably close to genocide. The United Nations Convention on Genocide defines the crime as an act committed with intent to destroy, in whole or in part, a national, ethnic, racial or religious group. Article III of the Convention proclaims as punishable not only the act itself, but also conspiracy to commit it, incitement to it, attempts to perform it, and complicity in it. Article IV specifically insists that punishment applies to rulers, public officials or private individuals.

The Convention bears the date of 9th December 1948, and has been ratified by the United Kingdom and 75 other Governments.

It is, of course, assumed by Governments that preparation for nuclear war does not constitute conspiracy to prepare genocide. In Britain, those who physically resist the installation of weapons of mass-obliteration are normally charged with the offence of "breaching the peace", however pacific their protests may be shown to have been.

Things go no better in France, or Italy, or Federal Germany, or Czechoslovakia, or the Soviet Union. Private citizens who object to the deployment of the machinery of extermination are quite normally intimidated, and all too often actually restrained in prisons, in accordance with laws which are purely national, contingent, and subordinate to the near-universal force of the 1948 Convention.

There will, however, be no Nuremburg Tribunal to order the execution of the losers in the next war. All will lose, and among any survivors laws of any kind will be part of the same poisonous ruins as the material artifacts of civilisation. The most optimistic predictions about that war assume regression on a total scale, perhaps for centuries. Dependent upon the rigours of the conflict, worse prospects are commonly anticipated. It is by no means outside the technical scope of modern armourers to render the entire planet uninhabitable by people of any kind.

Not only are these things widely understood: they have penetrated people's minds in an insidious way, alongside the realisation that conscience, in the world which plans for holocaust, is itself an outlaw. As a result, authority all-too-easily overrides it. People in the main value order, and social harmony, however conscious they may be of injustice or institutional wrongs. People also value their loyalties to their own primary groupings, the very groupings under whose protection the Convention on Genocide attempted to place them. If the attempt to reach toward a wider, more comprehensive law of humanity is to succeed, then it will have to answer the United Nations, as an assemblage of nation states, with an equally general, profoundly popular, international movement.

This book is a partial account of an attempt to reach in this direction. It contains polemic descriptions of the problems posed by the world-wide arms race, and alongside chronicles some of the efforts made to link the European Peace Movements in a continuing international forum. Many people have contributed to this considerable labour, and many of them are named in the pages which follow. All of us come from different backgrounds, and we do not lack disagreements. What we share, however, is a priority which leads us continually closer to one another, and so these necessary arguments do far more to unite than divide us. As I have been confronted by the issues of which this book treats, I have been made more than ever aware of the truly collective labour of thinking which is necessary. I have been trying to follow the argument where it leads, and everywhere I have met others in the same predicaments.

Many of these people have given invaluable help in drafting the arguments which follow. My particular thanks are due to Perry Anderson, M.S. Arnoni, Michael Barratt Brown, Tony Benn, Robin Blackburn, Stephen Bodington, Phil Braithwaite, Ken Fleet, Peri Pamir, Tony Simpson and Tony Topham. All of them have taken great pains to help me avoid errors of fact and judgement, and I am deeply grateful for their help and comradeship. I am also very much indebted to Rita Maskery who has had these texts, and many similar ones on her typewriter for long hours at a time. But the greatest debt, owed by all of us, is to the resurgent peace movements which have rekindled hope where all that weaponry threatened to extinguish it. In particular, I have drawn inspiration from my colleagues who have made great sacrifices to create and maintain the Liaison Committee for European Nuclear Disarmament, which has gathered every two months in Brussels in order to organise three major conventions of the European peace movements. I would also like to express my gratitude to the Japanese and Pacific peace movements, and above all to the Venerable Sato of Gensuikyo, who has made a prodigious contribution to bringing together the separate efforts of pacifists and workers for disarmament around the world.

I hope these papers, which are working papers, will make their contribution to this growing common effort.

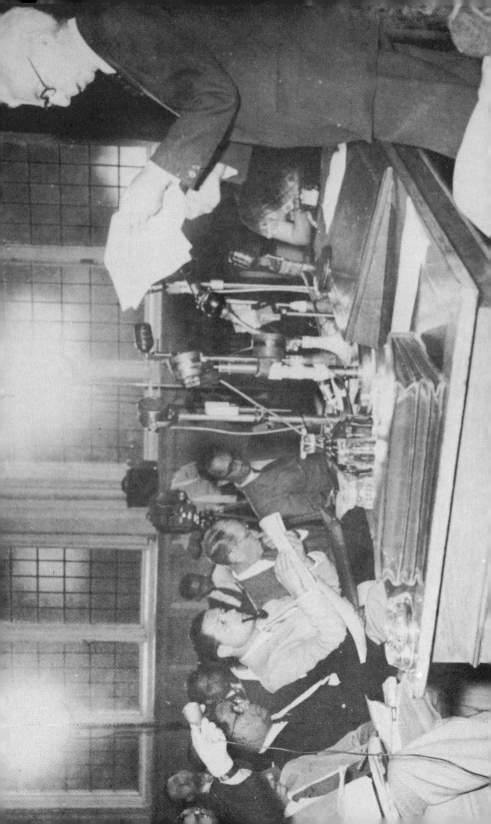

CHAPTER ONE

Bertrand Russell
and the Problem of
'Deterrence'

The new movement for nuclear disarmament in Europe, which has swept across the continent in the first years of the present decade, offers many similarities to the earlier peace movement, remembered now by people entering middle age.

In the late '50s and early '60s, however, life was rather simpler than it is today. The differences between the peace movements of then and now are perhaps as important as their similarities. So, too, are the differences in the contexts in which they seek to act.

In 1955, Bertrand Russell and Albert Einstein published the famous manifesto which launched the Pugwash movement, so named because the first international meeting of scientists which it called into being met at Cyrus Eaton's estate in Pugwash, Nova Scotia.

This document, reproduced below, sets out the classic statement of the perils of nuclear war, which, its authors established, might quite possibly put an end to the human race. Their judgement has lost none of its validity. But the political disputes which divide the world have changed significantly since Russell and Einstein agreed their text. "The world is full of conflicts", they wrote, "and, overshadowing all minor conflicts, the titanic struggle between communism and anti-communism". Two-and-a-half decades on, this "titanic struggle" has radically changed its form.

Even in 1955, anti-communism had many exponents, from quasi-feudal despots, to the directors of great capitalist corporations, to social democrats or libertarian socialists. Those opposing communism in 1980 represent a no less incompatible spectrum than before, although the shades of opinion included in it are now perhaps more finely delineated. On the other side, those supporting communism have fragmented into a dizzying variety of schools. There are Soviet communists, and Chinese communists; Albanians and Yugoslavs; Cubans and Euro-communists.

◀ *Russell speaking at Pugwash.*

Doctrinal disagreements follow these national and regional cleavages, and also, to some degree, overlay them. In capitalist countries, there are in the 1980s a kaleidoscope of small, and not so small, groupings reflecting and further fracturing these arguments. There are Trotskyists and Maoists, followers of Stalin and innumerable socialists who wish to find their way back to Marx.

Between actual states, these arguments have not remained verbal. Military exchanges have taken place between the USSR and China across a heavily armed frontier. A whole network of nuclear shelters was subsequently constructed in Chinese cities as a defence against possible Soviet attack. Soviet SS-20s ring China, just as they are also targeted upon Europe. Armies of the Warsaw Pact have intervened in force to change the policies and depose the Government of Czechoslovakia. Vietnam has invaded Cambodia, and established a puppet government to replace the communists of the Khmers Rouges, who are now accused in a worldwide public relations campaign of being as bad as, if not worse than, the Nazis. (The truth is their cruelties were much more reminiscent of those of Stalin than they were of any other regime.) China has invaded Vietnam and exacted heavy losses of life and materials in order to administer what her leaders have described as a "lessòn". It is unfortunately not entirely excluded that a second such "lesson" may follow. Following the example and teaching of Stalin in the Soviet Union, communist revolutions in China, Indo-China, and elsewhere have been integrally interwoven with nationalism, and while this powerful influence has at times increased their appeal to their domestic populations, it has also corroded the alleged internationalism of communism, producing in the end a variety of more or less overtly antagonistic "communisms".

Not a whit less divided is the capitalist world. Whilst multinational companies establish a new globalism, serious divisions of economic interest separate the United States from the most potent European nations, and there are widening breaches between both of these power centres and their dynamic competitors in Japan. If conventional socialist doctrines on imperialism are true, then the real world conflict is as likely to follow inter-capitalist fractures as it is to remain contained in the ideological rupture of the cold war. At the same time realistic "western" analysis can show that ideological quarrels have relatively easily become exchanges of shot and shell between "communist" states, whilst the basic East-West divide has remained frozen in an uneasy peace.

In the developing confrontation between the two great superpowers which followed the revolution in Iran and the Soviet invasion of Afghanistan, not only did many of the major communist parties declare themselves neutral to a greater or lesser extent, but one of the more significant dimensions of growing tension emerged in the increasingly apparent, if surely impermanent, alignment of American and Chinese interests. On the other side, fierce disputes have been carried on behind closed doors as different European states have contested the United States' attempts to impede the construction of a gas pipeline from the USSR.

All this has made the maintenance of peace immeasurably more difficult, since the complex of shifting affinities involves risk that where one dispute between two contenders might be negotiated to a settlement, the actions of a third party may serve to reopen old divisions on a new plane, or create new conflicts immediately after the resolution of existing ones. That more than one of the potential contenders phrase their communiques in the language of Marxism, with quotations from the same scriptures, by no means ameliorates this difficulty.

The fragmentation of interests within the blocs makes the old concept of detente infinitely more difficult to pursue. Even if all the statesmen in all the powers were firmly bent on avoiding war at all costs, they would require consummate expertise and skill to do so. However, it seems rather plain that peace is not exactly the first priority for all of them, so that the avoidance of war requires other advocates, with firmer commitments, if it is to be adequately promoted.

All this would have been a warning to heed even if each of the worlds of Russell and Einstein had simply subdivided: but in fact both parts of their world have also entered other profound crises. Fission has followed crisis, and aggravated it in the process. Apparent economic stability in the West has given way to deep slump, mass unemployment, and aggravated civil disorder in many countries. The once monolithic political conformity of the East has also broken into serial problems, promoting apathy, withdrawal and even non-co-operation on a wide scale. Strident dissidence has become evident among certain minorities. In both halves of this cold peace, troubles now come, not in single spies, but in whole battalions.

However complex the evolution of affairs since they wrote their manifesto, Russell and Einstein were right to pinpoint what has remained the unresolved problem of our time, to which we may find no simple solution in any scriptures, secular or other. In a prophetic moment more than a hundred years earlier, the authors of the Communist Manifesto had spoken of the class struggle (which they clearly saw as a democratic process in the fullest sense of the words), as ending "either in a revolutionary reconstitution of society at large or in the common ruin of the contending classes".

That "common ruin" now looms over us. It is no longer a question of socialism or barbarism, but of survival or the end of our species. Although this dilemma has confronted us since the Hiroshima explosion in August 1945, we have neither adequately understood it, nor have we yet resolved it. It will be more extensively discussed below.

Yet the existence of this dilemma does not at all annul the other lesser social tensions which demand real change in the structures of our societies, East and West alike. The inhibition of such change itself intensifies the threat of war, while the threat of war is used to reinforce that inhibition.

In his attempt to focus these prospects more than 20 years ago, Bertrand Russell drew three rather evident conclusions: first, that any future large-scale war would bring disaster "not only to belligerents, but to mankind"; second, that little wars would always henceforward contain the risk of becoming great, and that the more of them there were, the more likely it would be that one or another of them might grow to encompass our general destruction; and third, that even were existing nuclear weapons all by agreement to be destroyed, the outbreak of any future major war would ensure that replacements would be used as soon as they could be manufactured.[1] So far more than a hundred "little" wars have raged since 1945, and two of them, those in Korea and Indo-China, involved the use of a firepower more horrendously devastating than the totality of that available during the Second World War. To this matter, too, we shall return below. In one sense, this fact does not contradict what Russell said: war in Afghanistan, or in Iran, or in Eritrea, or in Namibia, or in the Lebanon, or who knows where next, does indeed carry the most fearful prospect of escalation, drawing in both active external sponsors and passive bystanders. In another sense, those who have preached the conventional doctrine of deterrence can be yielded (for what it is worth), their claim that ever-enlarging nuclear arsenals in both superpowers have up to now kept them apart from direct engagement one with another, and schooled them in exploring the delicate risks of proxy conflicts. The proxies will take no comfort from this.

This doctrine of deterrence has not stood still, however. Until recently, one of its most loyal British proponents has been Mr Denis Healey, who informed us in the early 1950s that the best guide to the true state of the world was Thomas Hobbes, who understood power politics. For Hobbes, fear was an indispensable component of the impulse to statehood, upon which depended the public peace and the containment of the "war of each against all", which otherwise raged in the society of natural man. But if this doctrine had been true, Hiroshima would surely have generated sufficient fear to force us all to accept the need for a genuinely international polity. It did not. Instead, it became an obstacle to such a polity. Deterrence theory, founded in one kind of technology, and within a given geo-political balance, has reiterated various rather primitively Hobbesian prescriptions to all who would listen, while both technologies and political realities have been borne along beneath it in a heaving flux of change. Hobbes himself would have been infinitely wiser than his modern epigones. He would never have ignored corporeal being because of a web of words. Order may once have been based on fear, but today fear has reached a point at which it imminently threatens to destroy what it has left of "order".

When Bertrand Russell sought to explain the confrontation of the nuclear superpowers, back in 1959, he offered a famous analogy:

"Since the nuclear statemate became apparent, the Governments of East and West have adopted the policy which Mr Dulles calls 'brinkmanship'. This is a policy adapted from a sport which, I am told, is practised by the sons of very rich Americans. This sport is called 'Chicken!' It is played by choosing a long straight road with a white line down the middle and starting two very fast cars towards each other from opposite ends. Each car is expected to keep the wheels of one side on the white line. As they approach each other, mutual destruction becomes more and more imminent. If one of them swerves from the white line before the other, the other, as he passes, shouts 'Chicken!', and the one who has swerved becomes an object of contempt. As played by youthful plutocrats, this game is considered decadent and immoral, although only the lives of the players are risked. But when the game is played by eminent statesmen, who risk not only their own lives but those of many hundreds of millions of human beings, it is thought on both sides that the statesmen on the other side are reprehensible. This, of course, is absurd. Both are to blame for playing such an incredibly dangerous game. The game may be played without misfortune a few times, but sooner or later it will come to be felt that loss of face is more dreadful than nuclear annihilation. The moment will come when neither side can face the derisive cry of 'Chicken!' from the other side. When that moment is come, the statesmen of both sides will plunge the world into destruction."[2]

I do not cite this passage out of piety. Russell's parable is no longer adequate. As we have seen, various things have changed since 1959. Some were beginning to change, at any rate in minds like Mr Henry Kissinger's, even before that time.

Some changes were rather evident to ordinary people, more or less instantly. Others were not. Within the game of "chicken" itself, we had the Cuba crisis of 1962. We shall discuss this later, but for our present purposes it is enough to note that Mr Krushchev swerved. This persuaded certain shallow advocates of the game that deterrence actually worked. But rather more significantly, it also persuaded the more faithful Hobbesians among Mr Krushchev's colleagues that considerably greater effort should be lavished on the perfection of a swerve-proof war machine. Consequently, the nuclear armament balance shifted, if not in the dramatic manner announced by Washington alarmists, at any rate in the direction of something closer to effective parity.

In addition to this, proliferation of nuclear weaponry continued. This is discussed below, and all that we need to say about it here is that it has complicated the rules of the game rather considerably. The French allowed if they did not actually encourage public speculation about the thought that their deterrent was more than unidirectional, if their putative defenders ever showed undue reluctance to perform, in time of need, the allotted role. The arrival of the Chinese as a potential nuclear force produced a new prospect of a three-way "chicken" game, with both main camps holding out at least a possibility that, in appropriate circumstances, they might "play the China card". But here the metaphor is mixing itself. Staying within the rules Russell advanced, we would have to express it like this: the Chinese "deterrent" could, at least in theory, be set to intervene against either of the other participants in the joust, unpredictably, from any one of a bewildering number of side-entries to the main collision course.

As if this were not problem enough, the war-technology has itself evolved, so that:

a. military costs have escalated to the point where nuclear powers are quite apparently increasingly impotent if they are barred from using what has now become by far their most expensive weaponry; and

b. nuclear weapons technique aspires to (although it may very well fail to meet) infinitely greater precision in attack. This brings nearer the possibility of pre-emptive war, which is a perfectly possible abrupt reversal of standard deterrence presumptions.

To these facts we must add another, of powerful moment:

c. the stability of the world political economy, which seemed effectively unchallengeable in 1959, has been fatally undermined by the collapse of the Keynesian world order, deep slump in the advanced capitalist countries, and growing social tension within the nations of the Soviet sphere of influence, who have not for the most part been able to evolve those democratic and consensual forms of administration which could resolve their political tensions in an orderly and rational manner.

In the interaction of these developments, we have seen the consolidation, amongst other delinquencies, of the doctrine of "limited" nuclear war. We can only reduce this veritable mutation in strategy to Russell's exemplary folk-tale if we imagine that each participant car in the game enfolds smaller subordinate vehicles, which can be launched down the white line at even greater speed than the velocity of approach of the main challengers. These lesser combatants can, it is apparently believed, be set loose on one another in order that their anticipated crashes may permit time for the principals to decide whether it might be wise themselves to swerve or not. Any desire of the small fry to change course is already taken care of, because they are already steered by remote control. Of course, the assumption is that those involved in the "lesser" combat will necessarily be destroyed. Maybe their destruction can save their mother vehicles from perishing, although careful analysts think it very much more likely not.

Stated in this way, the game has become even more whimsical than it was in Russell's original model. But stiffened up with precise and actual designations, it loses all traces of whimsy. The lesser vehicles in the developing game of "limited" war are all of Europe's nations. Whether or not their sacrifice makes free enterprise safer in New York, or allows Mr Brezhnev's successors time to build full communism (and we may well be agnostic on both scores) what is securely certain is that after it Europe will be entirely and poisonously dead, and that the civilisations of Leonardo and Galileo, Bacon and Hobbes, Spinoza and Descartes and, yes, Karl Marx, will have evaporated without trace.

Before we consider the project for limited nuclear war in a little more detail, it is necessary to unravel the conventional doctrine of deterrence somewhat further. Advocates of this schema will often repudiate the fable of the chicken game. "It is a malicious travesty", they will tell us. The vogue question which is then very commonly posed by such people is this: "you complain about the destruction of Hiroshima and Nagasaki: but would these events have taken place, if Japan then had the benefit of a possible nuclear response?" Let us worry this problem a little. First, some obvious points. Did the Japanese in this speculative argument possess an equivalence of weaponry or not? If they were nuclear-armed, but with a smaller number of war-heads, or inadequate delivery systems, it is possible that their retaliatory capacity could be evaluated and discounted, in which case the American attack would presumably have gone ahead. If, on the other hand, the American Government perceived that it might not avoid parity of destruction or worse, it would in all likelihood have drawn back. It might even have hesitated for fear of less than equal devastation. "Aha!" say the deterrent philosophers: "you have conceded our case". Well, hardly. We must first pursue it for a few steps, but not before pointing out that it has already become completely hypothetical, and already travesties many other known facts about the real Japanese war prospects in August 1945, quite apart from the then existing, real disposition of nuclear weapons. (There are some strong grounds for the assumption that the Japanese would actually have been brought to a very quick surrender if the nuclear bombardment had never taken place, or indeed, even had it not been possible). But for the sake of argument, we are temporarily conceding this special case of the deterrent argument.

Let us then see what happens when we apply it further. In 1967, the Indian Government exploded a "peaceful" nuclear device. Subsequently Pakistan set in train the necessary work of preparation for an answering technology. Since partition, India and Pakistan have more than once been at war. There remain serious territorial claims at issue between them. The secession of Bangladesh inflicted serious humiliation on the Pakistan Government. What possible argument can be advanced against a Pakistan deterrent? We shall instantly be told that the present military rulers of that country are unsavoury to a remarkable degree, that they butchered their last constitutionally elected Prime Minister, and that they maintain a repressive and decidedly unpleasant administration. It is difficult, if not unfortunately impossible, to disagree with these complaints, all of which are founded in reason and justice. But as co-opted theorists of deterrence, we must dismiss them. Our adopted argument is, that if India and Pakistan are to be held apart from their next war, the deterrent is necessary to both sides. Their respective moral shortcomings, if any, or indeed, if all that have ever been alleged, have nothing to do with the case.

Late in April 1981, Mr F.W. De Klerk, the mineral and energy affairs minister of South Africa, publicly admitted that his country was producing a quantity of 45 per cent enriched uranium, which announcement signified that South Africa had the capacity to manufacture its own nuclear armament. This news was scarcely electrifying, since a nuclear device had already apparently been detonated in the South Atlantic during the previous year, and it had therefore been assumed, almost universally, that the South African bomb already existed. What should the black African "front-line States" then do? Deterrence positively requires that Angola, Zimbabwe and Mozambique should instantly start work on procuring their opposing bombs. After all, South African troops have regularly been in action outside their own frontiers, and the very vulnerability of the Apartheid State makes it perfectly possible that serious military contests could break out over the whole contiguous zone. To prevent such war, the Angolan or Zimbabwean bomb represents a prudent and uncontentious investment.

We can say the same thing about the States of the Middle East. To them we might add those of Central America. Would Cuba have been invaded during the Bay of Pigs episode, if she had deployed nuclear weapons? To cap it all, what about Japan? Her experience, surely, would seem to be the most convincing argument for developing an extensive arsenal of thermo-nuclear war-heads.

Strangely, these arguments are not heard in Japan. President Mugabe has not voiced them either. Japan's people have not escaped the customary scissions which are part of advanced industrial society, but if one thing binds them together, it is a virtually unanimous revulsion against nuclear weapons. African States repeatedly insist that they seek protection, not by deterrence, but by the creation of a nuclear-free zone. Clearly they have not yet learnt the lessons which are so monotonously preached in the Establishment newspapers of the allegedly advanced nations.

If we were to admit that all nation States had an intrinsic right to defend their institutions and interests by all the means available to any, then nuclear proliferation would not merely be unavoidable, but unimpeachable within the deterrent model. And it is this incontrovertible fact which reduces it to absurdity; and argues that Russell was in fact right to pose the question as he did. Very soon the chicken game will not only have a cluster of three nuclear States at one end of the white line, and a single super-State at the other, with the Chinese already able to intervene from a random number of side routes: but it will shortly have from 12 to 20 other possible contenders liable to dash, quite possibly unannounced, across the previously single axis of collision.

For those who still believe that this dreadful evolution will be prevented by the treaty on the Non-Proliferation of Nuclear Weapons, we must offer three warning notes. First, the treaty's Review Conference of August 1980, held in Geneva, failed to agree any "certificate of good health" for its operation, because the nuclear powers had flouted all their solemn promises to scale down their own nuclear stocks. Critics of the treaty said from the beginning that its weakness derived from the fact that under it the nuclear weapons-holding States were assuming the right to police the rest. This could only acquire moral validity if they began themselves to behave according to the same rules which they sought to impose on others. At Geneva, the Review Conference demonstrated that no such behaviour had materialised. Secondly, visible evidence of the collapse of the treaty's framework has come from the military relationship between the USA and Pakistan since the invasion of Afghanistan by the USSR. Vast conventional weapons shipments to Pakistan have already taken place, and vaster ones are contemplated, in spite of the previous US policy which had withheld arms supplies of all kinds from any State suspected of breaching the non-proliferation treaty. If breaches are now condoned by superpowers wherever their own perceived interests at at stake, then the treaty is not merely dead, but rotting away. Thirdly, as an augury, we have the Israeli bombardment of Iraq, which shows what we must expect now that proliferation is effectively uncontrolled. It was, coincidentally, Mr Ismat Kitani of Iraq who presided over the Geneva Review Conference, and who warned that "the failure of the talks would damage world peace".

Deterrence, in short, was in the beginning, a bi-polar game, and it cannot be played in a multi-polar world. It is therefore collapsing, but the danger is that this collapse will result in universal destruction if alternative approaches are not speedily accepted. This danger arises because deterrence is a doctrine, a hitherto partially shared mythology, a mental scarecrow which may well lose all credibility before the material war potential which gave rise to it has even begun to be dismantled.

There was always, of course, a much simpler rebuttal of the doctrine. It is, was, and has always been, utterly immoral. Unfortunately, this argument, which is unanswerable, is not usually given even the slightest consideration in the world's war-rooms, although there is a fair deal of evidence that the people who staff these sometimes find it difficult to avoid traumatic neuroses about the effects of all their devilish labours.

However, the "lateral" proliferation of nuclear weapons to ever larger numbers of States, is by no means the most drastic process by which such weapons are multiplied. Lateral proliferation will provide more and more problems for the peace of the world, but the "vertical" proliferation of superpower arsenals is fearsome on an infinitely more dreadful scale. And it is the evolution of nuclear war-fighting doctrine and the preparation for limited nuclear war, which provides unquestionably the most serious threat we face in the 1980s, disturbed though rational men and women are bound to be by the prospects of the spawning of autonomously controlled atomic war-heads from one troubled region to the next. The "limited" nuclear exchange in Europe is likely to take place before one can be prepared on the Indian subcontinent, or yet in Africa. It is also scheduled to deploy as large a proportion of the firepower of the two great arsenals as may be needed.

How did we arrive at this mutation in strategic policy, which has begun to generate weapons designed to fight war rather than to "deter" it?

At the time when Bertrand Russell was campaigning for nuclear disarmament in Britain, there was an imbalance in the nuclear explosive stockpiles, although thermo-nuclear weapons already amply guaranteed the destruction of both superpowers, if they were to venture into war. According to Herbert York, the United States then had between 20 and 40 million kilotons of explosives, "or the energy equivalent of some 10,000 World War II's".

"We had reached" wrote York, "a level of supersaturation that some writer characterised by the word 'overkill', an understatement in my opinion. *Moreover, we possessed two different but reinforcing types of overkill. First, by 1960 we had many more bombs than they had urban targets, and second, with a very few exceptions such as Greater Moscow and Greater New York, the area of destruction and intense lethality that a single bomb could produce was very much larger than the area of the targets*. Since all, or practically all, strategic weapons were by then thermo-nuclear, it is safe to assume that those Soviet or Chinese cities which were equivalent in size and importance to Hiroshima and Nagasaki were, by that time, targets for weapons from 100 to 1,000 times as big as the bombs used in history's only two real demonstrations of what actually happens when large numbers of human beings and their works are hit by nuclear weapons."[3]

However, overkill has its limitations: bombs in the megaton class, York tells us, do not become proportionately more lethal as they get bigger. The size of the bombs "outruns the size of the target". This inevitably wastes much explosive power on "sparsely populated areas". Nonetheless, if the murderous effect of fallout is considered, even in the early '60s both superpowers could easily render the entirety of each other's territories intensely radioactive, and still have many unexpended bombs to spare.

The military doctrine which accompanied the perfection of this technology was one of the "massive retaliation", in words of Secretary Dulles, or later, "Mutual Assured Destruction" as Defence Secretary McNamara styled it. Although its advocates always insisted that this was a deterrent doctrine designed to prevent war, it did nonetheless, bear an undeniable relationship to Russell's game of "chicken", whenever conflict between the two powers entered the stage of open confrontation. But during McNamara's own period, the seeds of the new doctrine of "flexible response" were already maturing. The assumption out of which this notion was to codify itself was that different levels of nuclear escalation could be defined, permitting an American President a power to move through a spectrum of lesser types of nuclear strike before all-out mutual destruction became unavoidable. In 1964, Mr McNamara specifically mentioned the need for "flexible capability" in nuclear forces. In 1969, Defence Secretary Clark Clifford called for weapons which could be "used effectively in a limited and controlled retaliation as well as for 'Assured Destruction'."[4]

To be fair, this transition was accompanied by much lobbying from European statesmen. Henry Kissinger records some of it in his memoirs; and seeks to place much of the responsibility at the door of his European allies:

"A similar problem existed with respect to tactical nuclear weapons. One might have thought that if our strategic forces tended toward parity with the USSR and if at the same time we were inferior in conventional military strength, greater emphasis would be placed on tactical nuclear forces. This indeed was NATO's proclaimed strategy of 'flexible response'. But there was little enthusiasm for this concept within our government. Civilian officials in the State Department and the Pentagon, especially systems analysis experts, were eager to create a clear 'firebreak' between conventional and nuclear weapons and to delay the decision to resort to *any* nuclear weapons as long as possible. They were reluctant, therefore, to rely on tactical nuclear weapons, which they thought would tend to erode all distinctions between nuclear and conventional strategy.

A passage from a study on NATO's military options reflected this state of mind. This particular study was unable to find *any* use for nuclear weapons in NATO even though our stockpile there numbered in the thousands: The primary role of our nuclear forces in Europe, the study argued, is to raise the Soviet estimate of the expected costs of aggression and add great uncertainty to their calculations. Nuclear forces do not necessarily have a decisive impact on the likelihood or form of aggression, the study concluded. This was an astonishing statement from a country that had preserved the peace in Europe for over twenty years by relying on its nuclear preponderance. Nor was it clear how forces thought not to have a decisive impact could affect the calculations of a potential aggressor. It was a counsel of defeat to abjure both strategic and tactical nuclear forces, for no NATO country — including ours — was prepared to undertake the massive buildup in conventional forces that was the sole alternative.

To confuse matters further, while American civilian analysts deprecated the use of nuclear weapons as ineffective and involving a dangerous risk of escalation, our allies pressed a course contradicting the prevailing theory in Washington. They urged both a guaranteed early resort to tactical nuclear weapons and immunity of their territories from their use. Inevitably, discussions that had been going on since 1968 in the NATO Nuclear Planning Group began to produce serious differences of opinion.

This group had been set up by Secretary McNamara as a device by which our allies could participate in nuclear decisions without acquiring nuclear weapons themselves. Denis Healey, then British Minister of Defence, had explained his government's view when Nixon visited London in February 1969. In Healey's judgment NATO's conventional forces would be able to resist for only a matter of days; hence early use of nuclear weapons was essential. Healey stressed the crucial importance of making the Soviets understand that the West would prefer to escalate to a strategic exchange rather than surrender. On the other hand, NATO should seek to reduce devastation to a minimum. The Nuclear Planning Group was working on solving this riddle; its 'solution' was the use of a very small number of tactical weapons as a warning that matters were getting out of hand.

What Britain, supported by West Germany, was urging came to be called the 'demonstrative use' of nuclear weapons. This meant setting off a nuclear weapon in some remote location, which did not involve many casualties — in the air over the Mediterranean, for example — as a signal of more drastic use if the warning failed. I never had much use for this concept. I believed that the Soviet Union would not attack Western Europe without anticipating a nuclear response. A reaction that was designed to be of no military relevance would show more hesitation than determination; it would thus be more likely to spur the attack than deter it. If nuclear weapons were to be used, we needed a concept by which they could stop an attack on the ground. A hesitant or ineffective response ran the risk of leaving us with no choices other than surrender or holocaust.

But what was an 'effective' response? Given the political impossibility of raising adequate conventional forces, the Europeans saw nuclear weapons as the most effective deterrent. But they feared the use of them on their territories; what seemed 'limited' to us could be catastrophic for them. The real goal of our allies — underlining the dilemma of tactical nuclear weapons — has been to commit the United States to the early use of *strategic* nuclear weapons, which meant a US-Soviet nuclear war fought over their heads. This was precisely what was unacceptable to American planners. Our strategy — then and now — must envisage the ultimate use of strategic nuclear weapons if Europe can be defended in no other way. But it must also seek to develop other options, both to increase the credibility of the deterrent and to permit a flexible application of our power should deterrence fail.''[5]

It was in March 1974 that the new Defence Secretary, James Schlesinger, announced a comprehensive justification for limited nuclear war. Since then, although United States spokesmen, including President Carter himself, have havered backwards and forwards on this question, "flexible targetting" has apparently gone remorselessly ahead, and the concomitant doctrines of limited war have become military orthodoxy. It is this fact which rendered the revelation, in August 1980, of the contents of Presidential Directive 59 so unsurprising to the specialists. It is also this fact which had previously provoked British military leaders and scientific planners, like Lord Mountbatten and Lord Zuckerman, to unrestrained protest.[6]

Of course, military doctrine is an arcane science, and while specialists debated these issues they were accorded a respectful if distant, albeit widespread, apathy. But, as the practical conclusions of their debates became plain, public moods began to change. First, the project for an enhanced radiation (or "neutron") bomb brought home to a wide audience the apparent truth that war-fighting, as opposed to "deterrent" weapons were far advanced in preparation. Then, the Soviet installation of SS-20 missiles, which could strike European or Chinese targets, but not American ones, aroused concern not only among Governments. And finally, the NATO decision to "modernise" theatre nuclear forces in Western

Europe, by installing Pershing II missiles and land-based cruise missiles throughout Europe, brought forth a storm of objections, and the beginning of a new approach to European disarmament. Neither the Soviet, nor the American "modernisations" were uniquely responsible for this profound movement of opinion. Europeans had begun to perceive their intended role as victims: limited war in Europe meant that schedules were being evolved which made them prime targets. If any of them, on either side, were over-run, they could anticipate a double jeopardy: nuclear bombardment from the "enemy" while they were themselves a nuclear threat, followed by nuclear bombardment by their "allies" if anyone was left to hit. In this growing realisation, Europe began to generate a continental Resistance, from Scandinavia to Sicily, from Poland to Portugal. This epic movement is still in its infancy, but already it demands attention.

Already there have been two major gatherings of its supporters, at the Brussels Convention for Nuclear Disarmament held in July 1982, and at a second, larger, meeting which was held in Berlin from 9 May-15 1983. In 1984, a third Convention has been scheduled for Perugia, in July. There can be little doubt that Russell's ghost will draw encouragement from this widening response to the dangers against which he warned so cogently, and with such prescience.

Footnotes

Parts of this text appear in Heresies *(Spokesman, 1982). Other parts were included in the Introduction to Alva Myrdal:* The Dynamics of European Nuclear Disarmament, *(Spokesman, 1981).*

1. Bertrand Russell: *Commonsense and Nuclear Warfare,* London, Allen and Unwin, 1959, p.29.
2. *Ibid.,* p.39.
3. Herbert York: *Race to Oblivion — A Participant's View of the Arms Race,* New York, Simon and Schuster, p.42.
4. See Jerry Elmer: *Presidential Directive 59 — America's Counterforce Strategy,* Philadelphia, American Friends Service Committee, 1981.
5. *The White House Years,* Weidenfeld and Nicholson & Michael Joseph, pp.218-9.
6. *Apocalypse Now?* Spokesman, 1980.

The Russell-Einstein Manifesto

". . . remember your humanity, and forget the rest."

In the tragic situation which confronts humanity, we feel that scientists should assemble in conference to appraise the perils that have arisen as a result of the development of weapons of mass destructon, and to discuss a resolution in the spirit of the appended draft.

We are speaking on this occasion, not as members of this or that nation, continent, or creed, but as human beings, members of the species Man, whose continued existence is in doubt. The world is full of conflicts; and, over-shadowing all minor conflicts, the titanic struggle between Communism and anti-Communism.

Almost everybody who is politically conscious has strong feelings about one or more of these issues; but we want you, if you can, to set aside such feelings and consider yourselves only as members of a biological species which has had a remarkable history, and whose disappearance none of us can desire.

We shall try to say no single word which should appeal to one group rather than to another. All, equally, are in peril, and, if the peril is understood, there is hope that they may collectively avert it.

We have to learn to think in a new way. We have to learn to ask ourselves, not what steps can be taken to give military victory to whatever group we prefer, for there no longer are such steps; the question we have to ask ourselves is: what steps can be taken to prevent a military contest of which the issue must be disastrous to all parties?

The general public, and even many men in positions of authority, have not realised what would be involved in a war with nuclear bombs. The general public still thinks in terms of the obliteration of cities. It is understood that the new bombs are more powerful than the old, and that, while one A-bomb could obliterate Hiroshima, one H-bomb could obliterate the largest cities, such as London, New York and Moscow.

◀ *Einstein.*

No doubt in an H-bomb war great cities would be obliterated. But this is one of the minor disasters that would have to be faced. If everybody in London, New York and Moscow were exterminated the world might, in the course of a few centuries, recover from the blow. But we now know, especially since the Bikini test, that nuclear bombs can gradually spread destruction over a very much wider area than had been supposed.

It is stated on very good authority that a bomb can now be manufactured which will be 2,500 times as powerful as that which destroyed Hiroshima. Such a bomb, if exploded near the ground or under water, sends radio-active particles into the upper air. They sink gradually and reach the surface of the earth in the form of a deadly dust or rain. It was this dust which infected the Japanese fishermen and their catch of fish.

No one knows how widely such lethal radio-active particles might be diffused, but the best authorities are unanimous in saying that a war with H-bombs might quite possibly put an end to the human race. It is feared that if many H-bombs are used there will be universal death — sudden only for the minority, but for the majority a slow torture of disease and disintegration.

Many warnings have been uttered by eminent men of science and by authorities in military strategy. None of them will say that the worst results are certain. What they do say is that these results are possible, and no one can be sure that they will not be realised. We have not yet found that the views of experts on this question depend in any degree upon their politics or prejudices. They depend only, so far as our researches have revealed, upon the extent of the particular expert's knowledge. We have found that the men who know most are the most gloomy.

Here, then, is the problem which we present to you, stark and dreadful and inescapable: Shall we put an end to the human race; or shall mankind renounce war?[1] People will not face this alternative because it is so difficult to abolish war.

The abolition of war will demand distasteful limitations of national sovereignty.[2] But what perhaps impedes understanding of the situation more than anything else is that the term "mankind" feels vague and abstract. People scarcely realise in imagination that the danger is to themselves and their children and their grand-children, and not only to a dimly apprehended humanity. They can scarcely bring themselves to grasp that they, individually, and those whom they love are in imminent danger of perishing agonisingly. And so they hope that perhaps war may be allowed to continue provided modern weapons are prohibited.

This hope is illusory. Whatever agreements not to use H-bombs had been reached in time of peace, they would no longer be considered binding in time of war, and both sides would set to work to manufacture H-bombs as soon as war broke out, for, if one side manufactured the bombs and the other did not, the side that manufactured them would inevitably be victorious.

Although an agreement to renounce nuclear weapons as part of a general reduction of armaments[3] would not afford an ultimate solution, it would serve certain important purposes. First: any agreement between East and West is to the good insofar as it tends to diminish tension. Second: the abolition of thermo-nuclear weapons, if each side believed that the other had carried it out sincerely, would lessen the fear of a sudden attack in the style of Pearl Harbour, which at present keeps both sides in a state of nervous apprehension. We should, therefore, welcome such an agreement, though only as a first step.

Most of us are not neutral in feeling, but as human beings, we have to remember that, if the issues between East and West are to be decided in any manner that can give any possible satisfaction to anybody, whether Communist or anti-Communist, whether Asian or European or American, whether White or Black, then these issues must not be decided by war. We should wish this to be understood, both in the East and in the West.

There lies before us, if we choose, continual progress in happiness, knowledge, and wisdom. Shall we, instead, choose death, because we cannot forget our quarrels? We appeal, as human beings, to human beings: Remember your humanity, and forget the rest. If you can do so, the way lies open to a new Paradise; if you cannot, there lies before you the risk of universal death.

Resolution

We invite this Congress, and through it the scientists of the world and the general public, to subscribe to the following resolution:

> *In view of the fact that in any future world war nuclear weapons will certainly be employed , and that such weapons threaten the continued existence of mankind, we urge the Governments of the world to realise, and to acknowledge publicly, that their purpose cannot be furthered by a world war, and we urge them, consequently to find peaceful means for the settlement of all matters of dispute between them.*

Professor Max Born (Professor of Theoretical Physics at Berlin,

Frankfurt, and Göttingen, and of Natural Philosophy, Edinburgh;
Nobel Prize in physics).

Professor P.W. Bridgman (Professor of Physics, Harvard University;
Nobel Prize in physics).

Professor Albert Einstein.

Professor L. Infeld (Professor of Theoretical Physics, University of
Warsaw).

Professor J.F. Joliot-Curie (Professor of Physics at the Collège de France;
Nobel Prize in chemistry).

Professor H.J. Muller (Professor of Zoology at University of Indiana;
Nobel Prize in physiology and medicine).

Professor Linus Pauling (Professor of Chemistry, California Institute of
Technology; Nobel Prize in chemistry).

Professor C.F. Powell (Professor of Physics, Bristol University; Nobel
Prize in physics).

Professor J. Rotblat (Professor of Physics, University of London; Medical
College of St. Bartholomew's Hospital).

Bertrand Russell.

Professor Hideki Yukawa (Professor of Theoretical Physics, Kyoto
University; Nobel Prize in physics).

Notes

1. Professor Joliot-Curie wishes to add the words: "as a means of settling differences between States".
2. Professor Joliot-Curie wishes to add that these limitations are to be agreed by all and in the interests of all.
3. Professor Muller makes the reservation that this be taken to mean "a concomitant balanced reduction of all armaments".

CHAPTER TWO

For a Nuclear-free Europe

One day after Mr Francis Pym, the British Secretary of State for Defence, revealed his plans for the placement of 160 cruise missiles in Britain, Russian sources leaked a "captured" file from American commando headquarters in Europe. This had been stolen almost two decades earlier by a Soviet spy, US Army Sergeant R.L. Johnson. Johnson had later been apprehended by the FBI, and sentenced to 25 years in prison. His son subsequently shot him dead during a prison visit. Reporting this rather bizarre story, the *Sunday Times* (22 June 1980) gave a revealing glimpse, but no more, of what Major-General B.E. Spivy, director of J-3 division, had been organising for the "defence" of his European allies. Unsurprisingly, perhaps, his schedules included a budget for "pre-emptive strikes at hundreds of cities in the Soviet Union". But they also included numerous similar nuclear assaults on "places in neutral or friendly countries, to deny their resources to Soviet troops". The lists included named cities: "69 in Yugoslavia, 36 in Austria, 13 in West Germany, 21 in Finland and five in Iran". A more detailed report was later furnished in the *New Statesman* (27 June 1980). The documents, it explained, appear

> to contain over 2,800 targets — possibly double that number — throughout Europe and parts of the Middle East. The targets are not strategic and do not include missile silos, but consist for the most part of lists of airfields and other facilities . . . railway and highway bridges, railway marshalling yards and sidings, military headquarters and camps, troop concentrations, waterways, port areas, motorway junctions and major and minor airports . . .

The weapons designated for this work ranged from 2.5 kilotons to 1.4 megatons.

All this had been worked out back in 1962. At that time the US Air Force was ready to drop "18 to 20 thousand megatons of nuclear weapons in Europe and the USSR within a 24-hour

◀ *Copenhagen to Paris Peace March.*

period". Curious observers will note, so prolific was the armoury by the time of the early '60s, that it was thought prudent to assign it to such hitherto unanticipated targets as bridges and motorway junctions.

Up to the mid-1960s the United States had enjoyed a preponderating lead over the USSR in the numbers and refinement of its nuclear weapons. For this reason, during this time, Western military doctrine was based upon "massive retaliation". This much was always public knowledge. What was not public was the information that much of this "retaliation" was designed to forestall any regrettable tendency among allies or neutrals to be over-run. "Assured destruction" was openly defined by US Defence Secretary Robert McNamara as the capacity to eliminate up to one quarter of the population of the Soviet Union, and up to half its industry. But the proportion of the allied populations scheduled for similar elimination was not public knowledge during the years of those calculations.

Today, we have no way of knowing what secrets are locked in the military planning compounds in either the United States or the USSR. But from what is publicly known it is clear that Europe is in a far worse position at the beginning of the '80s than was even secretly thinkable 25 years ago.

1980 began with an urgent and concerned discussion about rearmament. The Pope, in his New Year Message, caught the predominant mood: "What can one say", he asked, "in the face of the gigantic and threatening military arsenals which especially at the close of 1979 have caught the attention of the world and especially of Europe, both East and West?"

War in Afghanistan; American hostages in Teheran, and dramatic pile-ups in the Iranian deserts, as European-based American commandos failed to "spring" them; wars or threats of war in South East Asia, the Middle East, and Southern Africa: at first sight, all the world in turbulence, excepting only Europe. Yet in spite of itself Europe is at the fixed centre of the arms race; and it is in Europe that many of the most fearsome weapons are deployed. What the Pope was recognising at the opening of the decade was that conflicts in any other zone might easily spill back into the European theatre, where they would then destroy our continent.

Numbers of statesmen have warned about this furious accumulation of weapons during the late '70s. It has been a persistent theme of such eminent neutral spokesmen as Olof Palme of Sweden, or President Tito of Yugoslavia. Lord Mountbatten, in his speech, warned that "the frightening facts about the arms race . . . show that we are rushing headlong towards a precipice".[1] Why has this "headlong rush" broken out?

First, because of the world-wide division between what is nowadays called "North" and "South". In spite of United Nations initiatives, proposals for a new economic order which could assist economic development have not only not been implemented, but have been stalemated while conditions have even been aggravated by the oil crisis. Poverty was never morally acceptable, but it is no longer politically tolerable in a world which can speak to itself through transistors, while over and again in many areas, starvation recurs. In others, millions remain on the verge of the merest subsistence. The third world is thus a zone of revolts, revolutions, interventions, and wars.

To avoid or win these, repressive leaders like the former Shah of Iran are willing to spend unheard of wealth on arms, and the arms trade paradoxically often takes the lead over all other exchanges, even in countries where malnutrition is endemic. At the same time, strategic considerations bring into play the superpowers, as "revolutionary" or "counter-revolutionary" supports. This produces some extraordinary alignments and confrontations, such as those between the Ethiopian military, and Somalia and Eritrea, where direct Cuban and Soviet intervention has been a crucial factor, even though the Eritreans have been engaged in one of the longest-running liberation struggles in all Africa: or such as the renewed Indo-China war following the Vietnamese invasion of Cambodia, in which remnants of the former Cambodian communist government appear to have received support from the United States, even though it only came into existence in opposition to American secret bombing, which destroyed the physical livelihood of the country together with its social fabric. A variety of such direct and indirect interventions owes everything to geo-political expediency, and nothing to the ideals invoked to justify them. Such processes help promote what specialists call the "horizontal" proliferation of nuclear weapons, to new, formerly non-nuclear states, at the same time that they add their pressure to the "vertical" proliferation between the superpowers.

Second, the emergence of China into the community of nations (if this phrase can nowadays be used without cynicism) complicates the old pattern of interplay between the blocs. Where yesterday there was a tug-o'war between the USA and the USSR, with each principal mobilising its own team of supporters at its end of the rope, now there is a triangular contest, in which both of the old-established contestants may, in future, seek to play the China team. At the moment, the Chinese are most worried about the Russians, which means that the Russians will feel a constant need to augment their military readiness on their "second" front, while the Americans will seek to match Soviet preparedness overall, making no differentiation between the "theatres" against which the Russians see a need for defence. It should be noted that the Chinese Government still considers that war is "inevitable", although it has apparently changed its assessment of the source of the threat.[2] (It is the more interesting, in this context, that the Chinese military budget for 1980 is the only one which is being substantially reduced, by $1.9 billion, or 8.5 per cent).

Third, while all these political cauldrons boil, the military-technical processes have their own logic, which is fearsome.

Stacked around the world at the beginning of the decade, there were a minimum of 50,000 nuclear warheads, belonging to the two main powers, whose combined explosive capacity exceeds by one million times the destructive power of the first atomic bomb which was dropped on Hiroshima. The number grows continually. This is "global overkill". Yet during the next decade, the USA and USSR will be manufacturing a further 20,000 warheads, some of unimaginable force.

World military spending, the Brandt Report on North-South economic development estimated, ran two years ago at something approaching $450 billion a year or around $1.2 billion ever day.[3] More recent estimates for last year show that global military expenditures have already passed $500 billion per annum or $1.3 billion each day. Recently both the North Atlantic Treaty Organisation and the Warsaw Treaty Organisation decided to increase their military spending annually over a period of time, by *real* increments of between 3 per cent and 4.5 per cent each year. That is to say, military outlays are inflation-proofed, so that weapons budgets will automatically swell to meet the depreciation of the currency, and then again to provide an absolute increase. It is primarily for this reason that informed estimates show that the world-wide arms bill will be more than $600 billion per annum or $1.6 billion each day very early in the 1980s.

As part of this process, new weapons are continually being tested. At least 53 nuclear tests took place in 1979. South Africa also seems to have detonated a nuclear device. New missiles are being developed, in pursuit of the ever more lethal pin-pointing of targets, or of even more final obliterative power. In 1980 the Chinese have announced tests of their new intercontinental missile, capable of hitting either Moscow or Los Angeles. The French have released news of their preparations to deploy the so-called "neutron" or enhanced radiation bomb, development of which had previously been held back by President Carter after a storm of adverse publicity. In the United States, the MX missile, weighing 190,000 pounds and capable of throwing ten highly accurate 350 kiloton (350,000 tons of TNT equivalent) war-heads at Russia, each of which will be independently targeted, with high accuracy, is being developed. The R and D costs for this missile in 1981 will amount to $1.5 billion, even before production has started. This is more, as Emma Rothschild has complained,[4] than the combined research and development budgets of the US Departments of Labour, Education and Transportation, taken together with the Environmental Protection Agency, the Federal Drug Administration and the Center for Disease Control. The MX system, if it works (or for that matter even if it doesn't work) will run on its own sealed private railway, involving "the largest construction project in US history".[5] It will, if completed, "comprise 200 missiles with 2,000 warheads, powerful and accurate enough to threaten the entire Soviet ICBM force of 1,400 missiles".[6] No doubt the Russians will think of some suitable response, at similar or greater expense. As things are, the United States defence budget from 1980-1985 will amount to one trillion dollars, and, such is the logic of the arms race, an equivalent weight of new weaponry will have to be mobilised from the other side, if the "balance" is to be maintained.

All this frenetic activity takes place at a time of severe economic crisis, with many Western economies trapped in a crushing slump and quite unable to expand civilian production. Stagnant or shrinking production provides a poor basis for fierce rearmament, which nowadays often accompanies, indeed necessitates, cuts in social investment, schools, housing and health. The price of putting the Trident system into Britain's arsenal will probably be outbreaks of rickets among our poorer children.

But military research takes priority over everything else, and the result is staggering. In the construction of warheads, finesse now passes any reasonable expectation. A Minuteman III multiple independently targetable re-entry vehicle (or MIRV, as such a vehicle is conveniently described) will carry three warheads, and each warhead has an explosive power of 170,000 tons of TNT (170 kilotons, or kt). A Minuteman weighs 220lb. The first atomic bomb ever used in action had an explosive force of 12kt, and it weighed four tons.

Miniaturisation of megadeath bombs has made fine progress. So has the refinement of delivery systems. This is measured by the standard of Circular Error Probability (CEP), which is the radius of that circle centred on the target, within which it can be expected that 50 per cent of warheads of a given type might fall. Heavy bombers of the Second World War, such as those which visited Hiroshima and Nagasaki, had a very large CEP indeed. The Minuteman III system expects to land half its projectiles within a 350 metre radius of target, having flown more than 8,000 miles to do it. The MX, if it goes according to plan, will have a CEP of only a hundred metres. Such accuracy means that it will be perfectly possible to destroy enemy missile solos, however fortified these might be. The Russians are catching up, however. Their SS18 and SS19 missiles are already claimed to have CEPs of 450 metres.

If rocketry has advanced, so too has experimental aviation. The Americans have already tested Stealth, an aeroplane which "is virtually invisible to Soviet radar". Critics say that invisibility has been purchased at the cost of multiple crashes, since the new machines are fashioned into shapes which are decidedly unfunctional for flying, in order to elude detection. Stealth is a fighter, but plans have been leaked (in the course of the American elections, during which, apparently, votes are assumed to be attracted to the most bloodthirsty contender) for a similarly-wrought long-range bomber. Officials in the US Defence Department insist that contorted shapes are only part of the mechanism which defeats radar detection: apparently new materials can be coated onto aircraft skins, to absorb radio waves. By such means, together with navigational advances, it may be hoped to secure even greater accuracy of weapon delivery.

Two questions remain. First, as Lord Zuckerman, the British Government's former chief scientific advisor, percipiently insists, what happens to the other 50 per cent of warheads which fall outside the CEP? The military may not be interested in them, but other people are. Second, this remarkable triumph of technology is all leading to the point where someone has what is politely called a "first-strike capability". Both the Russians and the Americans will soon have this capability. But what does it *mean*? It clearly does *not* mean that one superpower has the capacity to eliminate the possibility of retaliation by the other, if only it gets its blow in first. What it does signify is the capacity to wreak such destruction as to reduce any possible response to an "acceptable" level of damage. This is a level which will clearly vary with the degree of megalomania in the respective national leaderships.

All informed commentators are very wary about "first strike capability" because with it the whole doctrine of mutually assured destruction (appropriately known under the acronym MAD) will no longer apply. With either or both superpowers approaching "first strike" potential, the calculations are all different. Yesterday we were assured, barring accidents, of safety of a bizarre and frightening kind: but now each new strengthening of the arsenals spells out with a terrifying rigour, a new, unprecedented danger. Pre-emptive war is now a growing possibility. It is therefore quite impossible to argue support for a doctrine of "deterrence" as if this could follow an unchanging pattern over the decades, irrespective of changes in the political balance in the world, and irrespective of the convolutions of military technology.

In fact, "deterrence" has already undergone fearsome developments. Those within the great military machines who have understood this have frequently signalled their disquiet. "If a way out of the political dilemmas we now face is not negotiated", wrote Lord Zuckerman, "our leaders will quickly learn that there is no technical road to victory in the nuclear arms race".[7] "Wars cannot be fought with nuclear weapons", said Lord Mountbatten: "There are powerful voices around the world who still give credence to the old Roman precept — if you desire peace, prepare for war. This is absolute nuclear nonsense."[8]

Yet serious discussion of disarmament has come to an end. The SALT II agreements have not been ratified. The Treaty on the non-proliferation of nuclear weapons is breaking down, and the non-nuclear powers are convinced that all the nuclear weapon states are flouting it, by refusing to reduce their nuclear arsenals. It is true that following the initiative of Chancellor Schmidt talks will open between Senator Muskie and Mr Gromyko in order to discover whether negotiations can begin on the reduction of medium range arsenals in Europe. But unless there is a huge mobilisation of public protest, the outcome of such talks about talks is completely predictable.

In spite of detente, and the relatively stable relations between its two main halves during the past decade, Europe remains by far the most militaristic zone of the contemporary world.

At least 10,000, possibly 15,000, warheads are stockpiled in Europe for what is called "tactical" or "theatre" use. The Americans have installed something between 7,000 and 10,000 of these, and the Russians between 3,500 and 5,000. The yields of these weapons range, it is believed, between something less than one kiloton and up to three megatons. In terms of Hiroshima bombs, one three megaton warhead would have the force of 250 such weapons. But nowadays this is seen as a "theatre" armament, usable in a "limited" nuclear war. "Strategic" bombs, for use in the final stages of escalation, may be as large as 20 megatons. (Although of course those destined for certain types of targets are a lot smaller. The smallest could be a "mere 30 or 40 kilotons", or two or three Hiroshimas). Towns in Europe are not commonly far apart from one another. There exist no vast unpopulated tracts, plains, prairies or tundras, in which to confine a nuclear war. Military installations nestle among and between busy urban centres. As Zuckerman has insisted "the distances between villages are no greater than the radius of effect of low yield weapons of a few kilotons; between towns and cities, say a megaton".

General Sir John Hackett, a former commander of the Northern Army Group of NATO, published in 1978 a fictional history of the Third World War.[9] In his book this was scheduled for August 1985, and culminated in the nuclear destruction of Birmingham and Minsk. At this point the Russians obligingly faced a domestic rebellion, and everyone who wasn't already dead lived happily ever after. The General, as is often the case, knows a lot about specialised military matters, but very little about the sociology of communism, and not much more about the political sociology of his own side. Of course, rebellions are very likely in every country which faces the immediate prospect of nuclear war, which is why the British Government has detailed contingency plans for the arrest of large numbers of "subversives" when such a war is about to break out. (These may be discovered, in part, by reference to the secret County War Plans which have been prepared on Government instructions, to cope with every problem from water rationing to the burial of the uncountable dead). But there is no good reason to imagine that subversives are harder to arrest in the USSR than they are in Britain, to put the matter very mildly. Nor is there any very good reason to think that the Soviet Union stands on the brink of revolution, or that such revolution would be facilitated by nuclear war. The contrary may be the case. General Hackett's novel has Poles tearing non-existent communist insignia out of their national flag, and contains a variety of other foibles of the same kind: but we may assume that when it speaks of NATO, it gets things broadly right.

The General discusses the basis of NATO strategy which is known as the "Triad". This is a "combination of conventional defence, battlefield nuclear weapons and strategic nuclear action in closely coupled sequence". Ruefully, General Hackett continues "This was as fully endorsed in the United Kingdom as anywhere else in the Alliance. How far it was taken seriously anywhere is open to argument. There is little evidence that it was ever taken seriously in the UK . . . an observer of the British Army's deployment, equipment and training could scarcely fail to conclude that, whatever happened, the British did not expect to have to take part in a tactical nuclear battle at all . . ."[10]

General Hackett's judgements here are anything but fictional ones. The Earl Mountbatten, in the acutely subversive speech to which we have already referred, spoke of it in the most disparaging terms. If a former Chief of Staff and one-time Chairman of NATO's Military Committee found the idea unbelievable, this is strong evidence that General Hackett is quite right that NATO's basic strategy was indeed not "taken seriously" in the UK. Yet the doctrine of "flexible response" binds the UK while it remains in force in NATO, because it is enshrined in NATO's 1975 statement for Ministerial Guidance, in article 4:

"4. The long-range defence concept supports agreed NATO strategy by calling for a balanced force structure of interdependent strategic nuclear, theatre nuclear and conventional force capabilities. Each element of this Triad performs a unique role; in combination they provide mutual support and reinforcement. No single element of the Triad can substitute for another. The concept also calls for the modernisation of both strategic and theatre nuclear capabilities; however, major emphasis is placed on maintaining and improving Alliance conventional forces."

Article 11b develops this beyond any possible ambiguity:

"b) the purpose of the tactical nuclear capability is to enhance the deterrent and defensive effect of NATO's forces against large-scale conventional attack, and to provide a deterrent against the expansion of limited conventional attacks and the possible use of tactical nuclear weapons by the aggressor. Its aim is to convince the aggressor that any form of attack on NATO could result in very serious damage to his own forces, and to emphasise the dangers implicit in the continuance of a conflict by presenting him with the risk that such a situation could escalate beyond his control up to all-out nuclear war. Conversely, this capability should be of such a nature that control of the situation would remain in NATO hands.''

Yet so jumpy and jittery are military techniques, and so rapidly does their leapfrog bring both superpowers to the unleashing of ever newer devices, that the settled NATO principles of 1975 were already, in 1979, being qualified:

"All the elements of the NATO Triad of strategic, theatre nuclear, and conventional forces are in flux. At the strategic level, with or without SALT, the US is modernising each component of its strategic forces. And, as will be described below, the other two legs of the Triad are being modernised as well.

Integral to the doctrine of flexible response, theatre nuclear forces provide the link between US strategic power and NATO conventional forces — a link that, in the view of many, poses the ultimate deterrent against a European war.

With Strategic parity codified in the recent SALT II agreement, and with major Soviet theatre deployments such as the Backfire bomber and the SS20 missile, some have perceived a loose rung near the top of the flexible response ladder. Thus, consideration is being given to new weapons systems: Pershing II, a nuclear-armed ground-launched cruise missile (GLCM), and a new mobile medium-range ballistic missile (MRBM)."[11]

This fateful decision came at the end of a long process of other decisions, beginning with Richard Nixon's arrival in the United States Presidency. So it was that NATO finally determined, at the end of 1979, upon the installation of nearly 600 new *Pershing II* and *Tomahawk* (cruise) missiles.[12] The cruise missiles are low-flying pilotless planes, along the lines of the "doodlebugs" which were sent against Britain in the last years of Hitler's blitzkrieg, only now refined to the highest degree, with computerised guidance which aspires to considerable accuracy. And, of course, they are each intended to take a nuclear bomb for a distance of 2,000 miles, and to deliver it within a very narrowly determined area. There is a lot of evidence that in fact they don't work in the manner intended, but this will increase no-one's security, because it merely means that they will hit the wrong targets. Some of these might easily be located on "our" side.

President Nixon propounded the doctrine of limited nuclear war in his *State of the World* message of 1971. The USA, he said, needed to provide itself with "alternatives appropriate to the nature and level of the provocation . . . without necessarily having to resort to mass destruction''.

The conventional notion of deterrence had always been wrapped in swathes of assurances by its proponents that the actual use of nuclear weapons was unthinkable. This had been apparently borne out during the Cuba crisis, of which we have already spoken, when, as one American commentator put it, "we were eyeball to eyeball with the Russians, and they blinked''.[13] But in today's world, with nuclear forces in the superpowers at near parity, nowadays *Time* magazine offers up the pious hope that, next time, both parties might blink once. Meantime, so vast are the investments tied into the manufacture of nuclear warheads and their delivery systems that, in any real war, it is not their use but their non-use which has become "unthinkable". Since we must still presume that neither major power really wishes to destroy the world, we may begin to understand why more and more weight has therefore been placed on the notion of "theatre" weapons, which it is canvassed, might be actually employed without annihilating the whole of civilisation.

This is the most urgent of the unlooked-for transformations which have come over the logic of deterrence. It followed the development of highly accurate, adaptable and lethal weapons delivery systems. Now this threatens the very survival of European civilisation. In that crucial last speech of his, to the Stockholm International Peace Research Institute, the Earl Mountbatten seized the heart of the question:

> "It was not long, however, before smaller nuclear weapons of various designs were produced and deployed for use in what was assumed to be a tactical or theatre war. The belief was that there were hostilities ever to break out in Western Europe, such weapons could be used in field warfare without triggering an all-out nuclear exchange leading to the final holocaust.
>
> *I have never found this idea credible* (my italics). I have never been able to accept the reasons for the belief that any class of nuclear weapons can be categorised in terms of their tactical or strategic purposes."[14]

Lord Zuckerman has also declared that he sees no military reality in what is now referred to as tactical or theatre warfare.[15] "I do not believe," he told a Pugwash symposium in Canada,

> "that nuclear weapons could be used in what is now fashionably called a 'theatre war'. I do not believe that any scenario exists which suggests that nuclear weapons could be used in field warfare between two nuclear states without escalation resulting. I know of several such exercises.

They all lead to the opposite conclusion. There is no Marquis of Queensbury who would be holding the ring in a nuclear conflict. I cannot see teams of physicists attached to military staffs who would run to the scene of a nuclear explosion and then back to tell their local commanders that the radiation intensity of a nuclear strike by the other side was such and such, and that therefore the riposte should be only a weapon of equivalent yield. If the zone of lethal or wounding neutron radiation of a so-called neutron bomb would have, say, a radius of half a kilometre, the reply might well be a 'dirty' bomb with the same zone of radiation, but with a much wider area of devastation due to blast and fire."[16]

Pressure from the Allies has meant that Presidential statements on the issue of limited war have swung backwards and forwards. At times President Carter gave the impression that he was opposed to the doctrine. But the revelation of "directive 59" in August 1980 showed that there was in fact a continuous evolution in US military policy, apparently regardless of political hesitations by Governments. Directive 59 was a flat-out regression to the pure Nixon doctrine. As the *New York Times* put it:

"(Defence Secretary) Brown seems to expand the very meaning of deterrence alarmingly. Typically, advocates of flexible targeting argue that it will deter a sneak attack. But Brown's speech says the new policy is also intended to deter a variety of lesser aggressions . . . including conventional military aggression . . ."

Obviously, as the NYT claims, this is liable to

"increase the likelihood that nuclear weapons will be used."[17]

Where would such weapons be used? That place would experience total annihilation, and in oblivion would be unable to consider the nicety of "tactical" or "strategic" destruction. If "limited" nuclear exchanges mean anything at all, the only limitation which is thinkable is their restriction to a particular zone. And that is precisely why politicians in the United States find "limited" war more tolerable than the other sort, because it leaves a hope that escalation to the total destruction of both superpowers might be a second-stage option to be deferred during the negotiations which could be undertaken while Europe burns. It does not matter whether the strategists are right in their assumptions or not. There are strong reasons why a Russian counter-attack ought (within the lights of the Soviet authorities) to be directed at the USA as well as Europe, if Soviet military strategists are as thoughtful as we may presume. But the very fact that NATO is being programmed to follow this line of action means that Europeans must awaken to understand the sinister change that has taken place, beneath the continuing official chatter about "deterrence".

The fact that current Soviet military planning speaks a different language does not in the least imply that Europe can escape this dilemma. If one side prepares for a "theatre" war in our continent, the other will, if and when necessary, respond, whether or not it accepts the protocol which is proposed for the orderly escalation of annihilation from superpower peripheries to superpower centres. The material reality which will control events is the scope and range of the weapons deployed: and the very existence of tens of thousands of theatre weapons implies, in the event of war, that there will be a "theatre war". There may be a "strategic" war as well, in spite of all plans to the contrary. It will be too late for Europe to know or care.

All those missiles and bombs could never be used in Europe without causing death and destruction on a scale hitherto unprecedented and inconceivable. The continent would become a hecatomb, and in it would be buried, not only tens, hundreds of millions of people, but also the remains of a civilisation. If some Europeans survived, in Swiss shelters or British Government bunkers, they would emerge to a cannibal universe in which every humane instinct had been cauterised. Like the tragedy of Cambodia, only on a scale greatly wider and more profound, the tragedy of post-nuclear Europe would be lived by a mutilated people, prone to the most restrictive and destructive xenophobia, ganging for support into pathetic strong-arm squads in order to club a survival for themselves out of the skulls of others, and fearful of their own shadows. The worlds which came into being in the Florentine renaissance would have been totally annulled, and not only the monuments would be radioactive. On such deathly foundations, "communism" may be installed, in the Cambodian manner, or some other more primary anarchies or brutalisms may maintain a hegemony of sorts. What is plain is that any and all survivors of a European theatre war will look upon the days before the holocaust as a golden age, and hope will have become, quite literally, a thing of the past.

This carnivorous prospect is not at all identical with the simple supposition with which supporters of nuclear disarmament are often (wrongly) credited, that "one day deterrence will not work".

It rather implies that there has been a mutation in the concept of deterrence itself, with grisly consequences for us. In fact, deterrence is now so very costly that "conventional" responses are becoming impossible, to the point where even superpowers find themselves stalemated unless they are willing to discover means of "conventionalising" and then actually employing parts of their nuclear arsenals. If the powers want to have a bit of a nuclear war, they will want to have it away from home.

It we do not wish to be their hosts for such a match, then, regardless of whether they are right or wrong in supposing that they can confine it to our "theatre", we must discover a new initiative which can move us towards disarmament. New technologies will not do this, and nor will introspection and conscience suddenly seize command in both superpowers at once.

We are looking for a *political* step which can open up new forms of public pressure, and bring into the field of force new moral resources. Partly this is a matter of ending superpower domination of the most important negotiations.

But another part of the response must involve a multi-national mobilisation of public opinion. In Europe, this will not begin until people appreciate the exceptional vulnerability of their continent. One prominent statesman,who has understood, and drawn attention to, this extreme exposure, is Olof Palme. During an important speech at a Helsinki conference of the Socialist International, he issued a strong warning:

> "Europe is no special zone where peace can be taken for granted. In actual fact, it is at the centre of the arms race. Granted, the general assumption seems to be that any potential military conflict between the superpowers is going to start some place other than in Europe. But even if that were to be the case, we would have to count on one or the other party — in an effort to gain supremacy — trying to open a front on our continent, as well. As Alva Myrdal has recently pointed out, a war can simply be transported here, even though actual causes for war do not exist. Here there is a ready theatre of war. Here there have been great military forces for a long time. Here there are programmed weapons all ready for action . . ."[18]

Basing himself on this recognition, Mr Palme recalled various earlier attempts to create, in North and Central Europe, nuclear-free zones, from which, by agreement, all warheads were to be excluded. (We shall look at the history of these proposals below.) He then drew a conclusion of historic significance, which provides the most real, and most hopeful, possibility of generating a truly continental opposition to this continuing arms race:

> "Today more than ever there is, in my opinion, every reason to go on working for a nuclear-free zone. *The ultimate objective of these efforts should be a nuclear-free Europe* (my italics). The geographical area closest at hand would naturally be Northern and Central Europe. If these areas could be freed from the nuclear weapons stationed there today, the risk of total annihilation in case of a military conflict would be reduced.

Olof Palme's initiative was launched exactly a month before the 1978 United Nations Special Session on Disarmament, which gave rise to a Final Document that is a strong, if tacit, indictment of the frenetic arms race which has actually accelerated sharply since it was agreed. A World Disarmament Campaign was launched in 1980 by Lord Noel Baker and Lord Brockway, and a comprehensive cross-section of voluntary peace organisations: it had the precise intention of securing the implementation of this Document. But although the goal of the UN Special Session was "general and complete disarmament", as it should have been, it is commonly not understood that this goal was deliberately coupled with a whole series of intermediate objectives, including Palme's own proposals. Article 33 of the statement reads:

> The establishment of nuclear-weapon-free zones on the basis of agreements or arrangements freely arrived at among the States of the zone concerned, and the full compliance with those agreements or arrangements, thus ensuring that the zones are genuinely free from nuclear weapons, and respect for such zones by nuclear-weapon States, constitute an important disarmament measure.[19]

Later, the declaration goes on to spell out this commitment in considerable detail.

Article 63 of this final document schedules several areas for consideration as nuclear-free zones. They include Africa, where the Organisation of African Unity has resolved upon "the denuclearisation of the region", but also the Middle East and South Asia, which are listed alongside South and Central America, whose pioneering treaty offers a possible model for others to follow. This is the only populous area to have been covered by an existing agreement, which was concluded in the Treaty of Tlatelolco (a suburb of Mexico City), opened for signature from February 1967.

There are other zones which are covered by more or less similar agreements. Conservationists will be pleased that they include Antarctica, the Moon, outer space, and the seabed. Two snags exist in this respect. One is that the effectiveness of the agreed arrangements is often questioned. The other is that if civilisation is destroyed, the survivors may not be equipped to establish themselves comfortably in safe havens among penguins or deep-sea plants and fish, leave alone upon the Moon.

That is why a Martian might be surprised by the omission of Europe from the queue of continents (Africa, Near Asia, the Far East all in course of pressing; and Latin America, with the exception of Cuba, already having agreed) to negotiate coverage within nuclear-free zones. If Europe is the most vulnerable region, the prime risk, with a dense concentration of population, the most developed and destructible material heritage to lose, and yet no obvious immediate reasons to go to war, why is there any hesitation at all about making Olof Palme's "ultimate objective" into an immediate and urgent demand?

If we are agreed that "it does not matter where the bombs come from", there is another question which is more pertinent. This is: where will they be sent to? Clearly, high-priority targets are all locations from which response might otherwise issue. There is therefore a very strong advantage for all Europe if "East" and "West", in terms of the deployment of nuclear arsenals, can literally and rigorously become coterminous with "USA" and "USSR". This would not in one step liquidate the alliances, or end all the tension. But it would constitute a significant pressure on the superpowers, since each would thenceforward have a priority need to target on the silos of the other, and the present logic of "theatre" thinking would all be reversed. None of this would lift the threat of apocalypse, but it would be a first step in that direction. As things are, we are in the theatre, and they are hoping to be able to watch us burn on their videos.

Nuclear-free Zones in Europe

If Europe as a whole has not hitherto raised the issue of its possible denuclearisation, there have been a number of efforts to sanitise smaller regions within the continent.

The idea that groups of nations in particular areas might agree to forgo the manufacture or deployment of nuclear weapons, and to eschew research into their production, was first seriously mooted in the second half of the 1950s. In 1956, the USSR attempted to open discussions on the possible restriction of armaments, under inspection, and the prohibition of nuclear weapons within both German states and some adjacent countries. The proposal was discussed in the Disarmament Sub-Committee of the United Nations, but it got no further. But afterwards the Foreign Secretary of Poland, Adam Rapacki, took to the Twelfth Session of the UN General Assembly a plan to outlaw both the manufacture and the harbouring of nuclear arsenals in all the territories of Poland, Czechoslovakia, the German Democratic Republic and the Federal German Republic. The Czechoslovaks and East Germans quickly endorsed this suggestion.

Rapacki's proposals would have come into force by four separate unilateral decisions of each relevant government. Enforcement would have been supervised by a commission drawn from NATO countries, Warsaw Pact adherents, and non-aligned states. Inspection posts, with a system of ground and air controls, were to be established to enable the commission to function. Subject to this supervision, neither nuclear weapons, nor installations capable of harbouring or servicing them, nor missile sites, would have been permitted in the entire designated area. Nuclear powers were thereupon expected to agree not to use nuclear weapons against the denuclearized zone, and not to deploy their own atomic warheads with any of their conventional forces stationed within it.

The plan was rejected by the NATO powers, on the grounds, first, that it did nothing to secure German reunification and, second, that it failed to cover the deployment of conventional armaments. In 1958, therefore, Rapacki returned with modified proposals. Now he suggested a phased approach. In the beginning, nuclear stockpiles would be frozen at their existing levels within the zone. Later, the removal of these weapon stocks would be accompanied by controlled and mutually agreed reductions in conventional forces. This initiative, too, was rejected.

Meantime, in 1957, Romania proposed a similar project to denuclearise the Balkans. This plan was reiterated in 1968, and again in 1972.

In 1959, the Irish government outlined a plan for the creation of nuclear-free zones throughout the entire planet, which were to be developed region by region. In the same year the Chinese People's Republic suggested that the Pacific Ocean and all Asia be constituted a nuclear-free zone, and in 1960 various African states elaborated similar proposals for an All-African agreement. (These were re-tabled in 1965, and yet again in 1974.)

In 1962 the Polish government offered yet another variation on the Rapacki Plan, which would have maintained its later notion of phasing, but which would now have permitted other European nations to join in if they wished to extend the original designated area. In the first stage, existing levels of nuclear weaponry and rocketry would be frozen, prohibiting the creation of new bases. Then, as in the earlier version, nuclear and conventional armaments would be progressively reduced according to a negotiated timetable. The rejection of this 1962 version was the end of the Rapacki proposals, but they were followed in 1964 by the so-called "Gomulka" plan, which was designed to affect the same area, but which offered more restricted goals.

Although the main NATO powers displayed no real interest in all these efforts, they did arouse some real concern and sympathy in Scandinavia. As early as October 1961, the Swedish government tabled what became known as the Undén Plan (named after Sweden's Foreign Minister) at the First Committee of the UN General Assembly. This supported the idea of nuclear-free zones and a "non-atomic club", and advocated their general acceptance. Certain of its proposals, concerning non-proliferation and testing, were adopted by the General Assembly. But the Undén Plan was never realised, because the USA and others maintained at the time that nuclear-free zones were an inappropriate approach to disarmament, which could only be agreed in a comprehensive "general and complete" decision. Over and again this most desirable end has been invoked to block any less total approach to discovering any practicable means by which it might be achieved.

In 1963, President Kekkonen of Finland called for the re-opening of talks on the Undén Plan. Finland and Sweden were both neutral already, he said, while Denmark and Norway, notwithstanding their membership of NATO, had no nuclear weapons of their own, and deployed none of those belonging to their Alliance. But although this constituted a *de facto* commitment, it would, he held, be notably reinforced by a deliberate collective decision to confirm it as an enduring joint policy.

The Norwegian premier responded to this *démarche* by calling for the inclusion of sections of the USSR in the suggested area. As long ago as 1959, Nikita Khrushchev had suggested a Nordic nuclear-free zone, but no approach was apparently made to him during 1963 to discover whether the USSR would be willing to underpin such a project with any concession to the Norwegian viewpoint. However, while this argument was unfolding again in 1963, Khrushchev launched yet another similar proposal, for a nuclear-free Mediterranean.

The fall of Khrushchev took much of the steam out of such diplomatic forays, even though new proposals continue to emerge at intervals. In May 1974, the Indian government detonated what it described as a "peaceful" nuclear explosion. This provoked renewed proposals for a nuclear-free zone in the Near East, from both Iran and the United Arab Republic, and it revived African concern with the problem. Probably the reverberations of the Indian bang were heard in New Zealand, because that nation offered up a suggestion for a South Pacific free zone later in the year.

Yet, while the European disarmament lobbies were stalemated, the Latin American Treaty, which is briefly discussed above, had already been concluded in 1967, and within a decade it had secured the adherence of 25 states. The last of the main nuclear powers to endorse it was the USSR, which confirmed its general support in 1978. (Cuba withholds endorsement because it reserves it rights pending the evacuation of the Guantanamo base by the United States.) African pressures for a similar agreement are, as we have already argued, notably influenced by the threat of a South African nuclear military capacity, which is an obvious menace to neighbouring Mozambique, Zimbabwe, and Angola, and a standing threat to the Organisation of African Unity. In the Middle East, Israel plays a similar catalysing role, and fear of an Israeli bomb is widespread throughout the region.

Why then, this lag between Europe and the other continents? If the pressure for denuclearised zones began in Europe, and if the need for them, as we have seen, remains direst there, why have the Governments of the Third World been, up to now, so much more effectively vocal on this issue than those of the European continent? Part of the answer surely lies in the prevalence of the non-aligned movement among the countries of the Third World. Apart from a thin scatter of neutrals, Europe is the seed-bed of alignments, and the interests of the blocs as apparently disembodied entities are commonly prayed as absolute within it. In reality, of course, the blocs are not "disembodied". Within them, in military terms, superpowers rule. They control the disposition and development of the two major "deterrents". They keep the keys and determine if and when to fire. They displace the constituent patriotisms of the member states with a kind of bloc loyalty, which solidly implies that in each bloc there is a leading state, not only in terms of military supply, but also in terms of the determination of policy. To be sure, each bloc is riven with mounting internal tension. Economic competition divides the West, which enters the latest round of the arms race in a prolonged and, for some, mortifying slump. In the East, divergent interests are not so easily expressed, but they certainly exist, and from time to time become manifest. For all this, subordinate states on either side find it rather difficult to stand off from their protectors.

But stand off we all must. The logic of preparation for a war in our "theatre" is remorseless, and the profound worsening of tension between the superpowers at a time of world-wide economic and social crisis all serves to speed up the Gadarene race.

The European Appeal

It was in this context that, at the beginning of 1980, the Russell Foundation joined forces with a variety of peace organisations in Britain (CND, Pax Christi, the International Confederation for Disarmament and Peace, among others), to launch an appeal to do precisely this.

An early draft of the appeal was written by E.P. Thompson. This was then circulated very widely in Europe, as a result of which a completely new draft was prepared incorporating the ideas of correspondents in many different countries, in Northern, Western, Southern and Eastern Europe. The appeal then took on its final form after a meeting in London in April 1980 at which French, British, West German and Italian supporters were present.

The appeal was announced at the end of that month and signatures were still being canvassed both in Great Britain and the rest of Europe up to Hiroshima Day, 6 August 1980. It calls upon the two great powers to "withdraw all nuclear weapons from European territory" and urges the USSR to halt the production of its SS20 missiles at the same time that it calls on the USA not to implement its decision to develop and install Pershing II and cruise missiles in the European "theatre". The aim is the removal of all nuclear air and submarine bases, nuclear weapons research, development and manufacturing institutions, and nuclear warheads themselves, from the whole continent, "from Poland to Portugal". This convenient slogan does not imply an unwillingness to negotiate the denuclearisation of European Russia, up to the Urals: it merely registers the existing real division between superpowers, East and West, on the one side, and the states of Europe, which are caught up in the effects of the arms race between those powers, like corks bobbing in the flood, on the other.

The initial response to what has already become known as the European Nuclear Disarmament movement was quite extraordinary. Thousands of people signed the launching appeal within a few weeks. It quickly became very evident that European hesitations about nuclear armament were in no way less developed than the reservations of Africans, Latin Americans, or Asians.

The British appeal soon gathered a galaxy of well-known names: more than 60 MPs, a number of representatives of Christian churches and peace movements, several peers, trade union leaders and a remarkable cross-section of men and women from the liberal professions. The composer Peter Maxwell Davies joined the painter Josef Herman with Moss Evans, the trade unionist. Melvyn Bragg, John Arlott, Glenda Jackson, Susannah York, and Juliet Mills of a new generation joined with earlier anti-nuclear campaigners like J.B. Priestley, Lord Brockway and Peggy Duff. But the growing swell of support included hundreds upon hundreds of other names which were not household words, but which reflected a real movement of opinion. Dockers, coalminers, students, housewives, busmen and computer programmers sent in the printed appeal forms, often affixed to home-made petitions listing dozens of adherents.

The approach to Europe was different. It was not possible and was not desirable for British activists to attempt to prescribe what courses of action were most relevant in all the different nations of the continent. Not only were the individual states within the two blocs quite different, one from another, but each of the important neutral states was caught in its own distinct patterns of affinities, from Yugoslavia, the inspirer of non-alignment, to Spain, recently emancipated from Franco, and poised before a variety of choices about possible future alliances. Facing up to this complexity, the Russell Foundation agreed to a proposal from Arthur Scargill to circulate the British appeal with a separate European call for a conference to elaborate whatever distinct approaches to continental disarmament might be practicable and necessary.

Already, as the British supporters were agreeing on their first moves, mass movements had grown up in Holland, Belgium and Norway. The Dutch and Belgians were able, in the swell of protest, to postpone the implementation of the NATO agreement to install cruise missiles in their countries. An important resistance was developing in Denmark. Very soon after the agreement of the text of the END appeal, contact between these movements took place. Key activists from each of these countries joined with eminent political leaders in supporting the proposed European Convention. In France, the END initiative was announced by Claude Bourdet, the editor of *Témoignage Chrétienne,* at a national press conference in Paris. Similar announcements were made in Oslo and Berlin at the same time, and a variety of organisations and individuals gave their support. From Spain, the well-known euro-communist spokesman Manuel Azcarate was joined by Dr Javier Solana Madariaga of the Socialist Party and by the distinguished Catholic writer Joaquin Ruiz-Gimenez Cortes, together with Joan Miró, the artist. An international meeting was organised by the Spaniards to ventilate the argument in the days before the recalled Helsinki Conference on European Security, scheduled to meet in Madrid in November 1980. Italian support was enthusiastic. An early signatory was Professor Giovanni Favilli, the scientist who had, from the beginning, been actively involved in the Pugwash movement. He happened to be a councillor in the city of Bologna, and in association with the town's mayor he convened meetings in all of the quartieri (or communal councils) of the region to consider the appeal, which was widely published in the civic journal and elsewhere. A Greek committee began to take shape, with the support of Andreas Papandreou, then opposition leader, amongst others. In Berlin, Professor Ulrich Albrecht, the peace researcher, gave extensive publicity to the appeal and gathered important support for it. At the same time, Rudolf Bahro, the East German author who had been imprisoned for publishing a book in the West and was subsequently deported after an amnesty, brought the adherence of the Green Party (with which he is currently working). Portuguese supporters included Ernesto Melo Antunes, the former Foreign Minister, and Francisco Marcelo Curto, Minister of Labour in the Soares government, alongside other members of Parliament. By mid-July there were supporters in Finland and Turkey, Hungary and Czechoslovakia, Ireland and Sweden. The roll-call reached from Roy Medvedev in Moscow to Noel Browne, the former Health Minister, in Dublin, and from Gunnar Myrdal in Stockholm to ex-premier Hegedus in Budapest.

The extensive response was reinforced by the encouragement of lateral appeals, in which groups in one country made direct appeals to similar groups in another. Several members of the British TUC General Council wrote to their opposite numbers in France, and a

British trade union group soon received approaches from Oslo. Members of British universities appealed to colleagues overseas. As the campaign gathers weight, this kind of initiative will gain importance, because it does not depend upon centralised networks of communications, and is a practical, as well as a symbolic, assertion of a growing all-European consciousness. Efforts were made to "twin" Cambridge and Siena, which for a time shared the burden of proximity to planned bases for cruise missiles. Such arrangements remain possible at a multiplicity of levels, between women's groups, churches, civic and industrial bodies, students, or a wide variety of sporting and cultural associations.

The problem of East-West contact may be especially susceptible to this kind of treatment. The appeal is quite specific about the need for such meetings:

> we must defend and extend the right of all citizens, East or West, to take part in this common movement and to engage in every kind of exchange.

At the same time, the appeal insists that:

> We must resist any attempt by the statesmen of East or West to manipulate this movement to their own advantage. We offer no advantage to either NATO or the Warsaw alliance. Our objectives must be to free Europe from confrontation, to enforce detente between the United States and the Soviet Union, and, ultimately, to dissolve both great power alliances.

No one should seek to minimise the difficulties involved in this task, but neither should they be magnified. On both sides of the European divide, and in the middle of it, there is a very considerable, and rapidly growing, awareness of the great folly of the arms race, which in the appeal is justly styled "demented". Whilst there are big differences in the scope for public campaigning in countries which support the two blocs, it is not possible for governments in either camp to ignore the pressure of informed and active public opinion in the other, still less when vast movements are developing a deliberate policy of lateral appeals to one another, and to the peoples of those nations as yet uninvolved in the campaign.

The movement for European nuclear disarmament, then, is a movement to transform the meaning of these blocs, and to reverse their engines away from war. If all previous efforts to denuclearise parts of Europe have foundered, this is in large measure because they have all been partial, and thus incapable of mobilising counter-pressures to dual bloc dominance on a wide enough scale. The paradox is that if President Ceausescu still wants a nuclear-free Balkan Zone, or if President Kekkonen still aspires to a de-nuclearised Baltic, then both are more likely to succeed within the framework of an all-European campaign than they would be in separate localised inter-state agreements. This is not at all to argue that de-nuclearisation might not come about piecemeal: of course this is quite possible, even probable. But it will only come about when vast pressures of public opinion have come into being; and these pressures must and will develop, albeit unevenly, over the continent as a whole. Europe is not Antarctica, but Europeans have at least as much right to live as do penguins.

For this reason, people must begin to organise, in a gigantic transnational campaign. If this task is difficult, postponement will not make it easier. A pan-European Convention will only be the beginning, although the organisational problems involved in this first step are large enough in all conscience. There must be meetings of many kinds, demonstrations, cross-frontier marches, concerts and festivals. We must melt the ice which binds our continent. Since, unlike governments, we possess no elaborate lasers or thermo-nuclear devices, we shall have to rely on more democratic powers: the light of our reason, the generosity of our hopes and the warmth of our love for one another. Europe is full of clever, resourceful and kindly people. When they reach out to each other, this daunting labour will shrink to human size, and solving it may then become simplicity itself.

Footnotes

Parts of this text have appeared in Smith and Thompson (eds): Protest and Survive *(Penguin, 1981). Other parts appeared in* European Nuclear Disarmament *(Spokesman Pamphlet No.72, 1980).*

1. *Apocalypse Now?* Spokesman, 1980, p.3.
2. Shortly after this text was first published, the Chinese Communist Party announced a revaluation of this judgement. War, they now thought, would happen if popular resistance to it proved insufficient to prevent it.
3. Estimates vary markedly, because it is difficult to know what values to assign to Soviet military production costs. If budgets are taken, then Soviet expenditure is apparently greatly reduced, because under a system of central planning prices are regulated to fit social priorities (or cynics might say, Government convenience). The alternative is to cost military output on the basis of world market or United States equivalent prices, which, since the USA still has a much more developed economy than the USSR, would still tend to

underestimate the real strain of military provision on the Soviet economy.

4. *New York Review of Books,* 3 April 1980: "Boom and Bust", pp.31-4.
5. Herbert Scoville, Jr: American's Greatest Construction: Can it Work? *New York Review of Books,* 20 March 1980, pp.12-17.
6. "The MX system can only lead to vast uncontrolled arms competition that will undermine the security of the US and increase the dangers of nuclear conflict", says Scoville.
7. *Apocalypse Now? ibid,* p.27.
8. *Ibid.,* p.13.
9. *The Third World War,* Sphere Books, 1979.
10. *Op. cit.,* p.50.
11. *NATO Review,* No.5, October 1979, p.29.
12. The acute problems which this missile has encountered in development makes an alarming story, which is told by Andrew Cockburn in *The New Statesman,* 22 August 1980.
13. *Time,* 23 June 1980.
14. *Apocalypse Now? ibid,* p.10.
15. *Ibid.,* p.21.
16. F. Griffiths and J.C. Polanyi, *The Dangers of Nuclear War,* University of Toronto Press, 1980, p.164.
17. Editorial, August 1980.
18. The text of this speech is reproduced in the Bertrand Russell Peace Foundation's *European Nuclear Disarmament — Bulletin of Work in Progress,* No.1, 1980.
19. This document is reproduced in *Apocalypse Now?,* pp.41-60.

European Nuclear Disarmament: a Manifesto

We are entering the most dangerous decade in human history. A third world war is not merely possible, but increasingly likely. Economic and social difficulties in advanced industrial countries, crisis, militarism and war in the third world compound the political tensions that fuel a demented arms race. In Europe, the main geographical stage for the East-West confrontation, new generations of ever more deadly weapons are appearing.

For at least 25 years, the forces of both the North Atlantic and the Warsaw alliance have each had sufficient nuclear weapons to annihilate their opponents, and at the same time to endanger the very basis of civilised life. But with each passing year, competition in nuclear armaments has multiplied their numbers, increasing the probability of some devastating accident or miscalculation.

As each side tries to prove its readiness to use nuclear weapons, in order to prevent their use by the other side, new more "usable" nuclear weapons are designed and the idea of "limited" nuclear war is made to sound more and more plausible. So much so that this paradoxical process can logically only lead to the actual use of nuclear weapons.

Neither of the major powers is now in any moral position to influence smaller countries to forego the acquisition of nuclear armament. The increasing spread of nuclear reactors and the growth of the industry that installs them, reinforce the likelihood of world-wide proliferation of nuclear weapons, thereby multiplying the risks of nuclear exchanges.

Over the years, public opinion has pressed for nuclear disarmament and detente between the contending military blocs. This pressure has failed. An increasing proportion of world resources is expended on weapons, even though mutual extermination is already amply guaranteed. This economic burden, in both East and West, contributes to growing social and political strain, setting in motion a vicious circle in which the arms race feeds upon the instability of the world economy and vice versa: *a deathly dialectic.*

We are now in great danger. Generations have been born beneath the shadow of nuclear war, and have become habituated to the threat. Concern has given way to apathy. Meanwhile, in a world living always under menace, fear extends through both halves of the European continent. The powers of the military and of internal security forces are enlarged, limitations are placed upon free exchanges of ideas and between persons, and civil rights of independent-minded individuals are threatened, in the West as well as the East.

We do not wish to apportion guilt between the political and military leaders of East and West. Guilt lies squarely upon both parties. Both parties have adopted menacing postures and committed aggressive actions in different parts of the world.

The remedy lies in our own hands. We must act together to free the entire territory of Europe, from Poland to Portugal, from nuclear weapons, air and submarine bases, and from all institutions engaged in research into or manufacture of nuclear weapons. We ask the two superpowers to withdraw all nuclear weapons from European territory. In particular, we ask the Soviet Union to halt production of the SS20 medium range missile and we ask the United States not to implement the decision to develop cruise missiles and Pershing II missiles for deployment in Western Europe. We also urge the ratification of the SALT II agreement, as a necessary step towards the renewal of effective negotiations on general and complete disarmament.

At the same time, we must defend and extend the right of all citizens, East or West, to take part in this common movement and to engage in every kind of exchange.

We appeal to our friends in Europe, of every faith and persuasion, to consider urgently the ways in which we can work together for these common objectives. We envisage a European-wide campaign, in which every kind of exchange takes place; in which representatives of different nations and opinions confer and co-ordinate their activities; and in which less formal exchanges between universities, churches, women's organisations, trade unions, youth organisations, professional groups and individuals, take place with the object of promoting a common object: to free all of Europe from nuclear weapons.

We must commence to act as if a united, neutral and pacific

Europe already exists. We must learn to be loyal, not to "East" and "West", but to each other, and we must disregard the prohibitions and limitations imposed by any national state.

It will be the responsibility of the people of each nation to agitate for the expulsion of nuclear weapons and bases from European soil and territorial waters, and to decide upon its own means and strategy, concerning its own territory. These will differ from one country to another, and we do not suggest that any single strategy should be imposed. But this must be part of a trans-continental movement in which every kind of exchange takes place.

We must resist any attempt by the statesmen of East or West to manipulate this movement to their own advantage. We offer no advantage to either NATO or the Warsaw alliance. Our objectives must be to free Europe from confrontation, to enforce detente between the United States and the Soviet Union, and, ultimately, to dissolve both great power alliances.

In appealing to fellow Europeans, we are not turning our backs on the world. In working for the peace of Europe we are working for the peace of the world. Twice in this century Europe has disgraced its claims to civilisation by engendering world war. This time we must repay our debts to the world by engendering peace.

This appeal will achieve nothing if it is not supported by determined and inventive action, to win more people to support it. We need to mount an irresistible pressure for a Europe free of nuclear weapons.

We do not wish to impose any uniformity on the movement nor to pre-empt the consultations and decisions of those many organisations already exercising their influence for disarmament and peace. But the situation is urgent. The dangers steadily advance. We invite your support for this common objective, and we shall welcome both your help and advice.

CHAPTER THREE

Nuclear-free Zones: Problems and Prospects

We have already referred to the United Nations Special Session on Disarmament, convened in New York in 1978, which excited world opinion by reaching agreement on the goal of "general and complete disarmament". This goal was deliberately coupled with a series of intermediate objectives. One of these concerned the establishment of nuclear-weapon-free zones. Article 33 of the final statement of the 1978 Special Session commends the idea of such zones "on the basis of agreements or arrangements freely arrived at among the states of the zone concerned, and the full compliance with those agreements or arrangements, thus ensuring that the zones are genuinely free from nuclear weapons, and respect for such zones by nuclear-weapons states, constitute an important disarmament measure".

Later the declaration goes on to spell out this commitment in a little more detail. It begins with a repetition:

> "The establishment of nuclear-weapons-free zones on the basis of arrangements freely arrived at among the states of the region concerned, constitutes an important disarmament measure,"

and then continues:

> "The process of establishing such zones in different parts of the world should be encouraged with the ultimate objective of achieving a world entirely free of nuclear weapons. In the process of establishing such zones, the characteristics of each region should be taken into account. The states participating in such zones should undertake to comply fully with all the objectives, purposes and principles of the agreements or arrangements establishing the zones, thus ensuring that they are genuinely free from nuclear weapons.
> With respect to such zones, the nuclear-weapon states in turn are called upon to give undertakings, the modalities of which are to be negotiated with the competent authority of each zone, in particular:
> a. to respect strictly the status of the nuclear-free zone;

◀ *Kurt Waldheim, UN Secretary-General.*

b. to refrain from the use or threat of use of nuclear weapons against
the states of the zone . . .
   States of the region should solemnly declare that they will refrain on a
reciprocal basis from producing, acquiring, or in any other way,
possessing nuclear explosive devices, and from permitting the stationing
of nuclear weapons on their territory by any third party and agree to
place all their nuclear activities under International Atomic Energy
Agency safeguards.''

Of course, the final document of the Special Session is not
beyond criticism. It is quite possible to identify a number of
problems to which the document gives no attention, or inadequate
attention. These become apparent even in the discussion about the
establishment of nuclear-free zones. But that discussion itself owes
a very great deal to the fact that agreement was reached in New
York in 1978 and although no-one would suggest that there now
exists a panacea for controlling and reversing the arms race,
nonetheless the Special Session has offered us a groundwork for the
development of nuclear-free zones.

There are two categories of involvement in nuclear-free zones.
First, the states constituting any such zone need to reach an
agreement about the commitments which are involved in nuclear-
weapon-free status, and to resolve upon means for jointly
enforcing that status. Second, the existing nuclear powers outside
such a zone need to be brought to an accord which can underwrite
it, by promising respect for its integrity. If the nuclear powers
refuse agreement to respect the zone, then it will not succeed in
establishing itself as much more than a propaganda commitment.
Important though such a commitment undoubtedly is, both the
First UN Special Session and the modern peace movement have
expected greatly more than this. It is, of course, always possible
that the nuclear powers could ratify an agreement concerning such
a zone, and then violate their own obligations. This possibility
raises very important problems, to the discussion of which we shall
return.

(1) The Agreement Between Members of a Nuclear-free Zone
Obviously every state which seeks the establishment of a nuclear-
free zone is seeking to share in an agreement prohibiting the
ownership, construction, acquisition, or use of nuclear weapons.
Such an agreement may find problems of definition in determining
what constitutes a nuclear weapon. Do ''nuclear weapons'' mean
weapons employing nuclear explosives, or can they include

weapons deriving their propulsion from nuclear fuels? Let us assume that this argument can be resolved: then we immediately require a whole series of definitions to control the meaning of other terms of the agreement. What is "ownership"? What is "construction"? "Acquisition"? Even, "use"?

Obviously the possession of nuclear weapons can involve a variety of real situations.. Some states own their own weapons, while others have developed a number of different relationships promoting the deployment of weapons belonging to others. The treaty for a nuclear-free zone will need to cast its net wide enough to forbid all of them equally. Weapons deployed directly or indirectly on behalf of a third party are, for the purposes of such an agreement, perhaps even worse than weapons directly owned and completely controlled by the party concerned. Each link in the deployment chain is liable to give rise to an uncertainty about use. A nuclear-free zone will obviously prohibit the placement of nuclear weapons in its agreed area, but most participants would presumably seek also to prohibit their co-signatories from owning and deploying such weapons in territories outside the agreed boundaries of the zone. Although this reservation seems far-fetched, there are several practical cases in which it is immediately relevant.

For example, some countries straddle boundaries. Turkey, for instance, is one. If Turkey were to seek to become a member of a European nuclear-free zone, would Turkish territory in Asia Minor be included? If it were not, consenting parties to the treaty inside Europe could imaginably be bombarded by Turkish-based nuclear weapons held outside the agreed boundaries of the zone. It seems fairly clear that no state could be allowed to occupy a schizoid position of this kind. The example of Turkey is not the only one in this category, and that is why the Soviet Union cannot simultaneously place part of its territory in, and part outside, a nuclear-free zone. This fact, not any lack of sensitivity to the "European" status of Russia, persuades many advocates of European Nuclear Disarmament of the advantage of the slogan of a "Europe free of nuclear weapons, from Poland to Portugal" rather than "from the Atlantic to the Urals".

A nuclear-free zone treaty would also have to define manufacture or construction in a clear and precise way. Every nuclear reactor is a potential hazard in this respect. If British nuclear power stations are supplying plutonium for the American nuclear weapons programme, then surely they are helping the "manufacture" of nuclear weapons. The British authorities deny such co-operation, saying that the plutonium which they supply to the United States goes there for civilian purposes only. But if the civilian use of British plutonium liberates American produced plutonium for the American military programme, is this not a specious quibble? States consenting to join a nuclear-free zone may wish to elaborate a framework which could clarify policy about such matters.

Let us assume that precise definitions of all these terms can be agreed. No signatory will make nuclear weapons or conduce to their manufacture, either on their own behalf, or in co-operation with any third party; no signatory will allow deployment of nuclear warheads or any other nuclear explosive machines, either on their own behalf or in co-operation with any third party; and no signatory will permit the transportation of nuclear weapons over their territory, including their territorial waters and their national air space.

It would be both reasonable and simple for the parties consenting to such a treaty to further pledge themselves to refrain from testing nuclear devices outside the territorial area covered by the treaty agreement.

Although it would not be by any means useless for existing non-nuclear powers to league themselves into nuclear-free zones, we may assume that some nuclear-free zones in Europe would be likely to include states which are at present deploying nuclear weapons of one kind or another within their national territories. If we could suppose that say, Austria, Switzerland and Yugoslavia were able to establish a nuclear-free zone treaty, this would undoubtedly exercise some persuasive influence in the other parts of Europe which are less fortunate in that their territories are already defiled by the presence of nuclear weapons. But if there is an agreement in the Central European zone or in the Balkans, either case will involve the physical withdrawal of nuclear weapons which are presently emplaced. Rather precise arrangements will be necessary to determine such withdrawal.

At the same time, members of a nuclear-free zone will need to decide how far they wish to extend their prohibitions to cover equipment which is ancillary to the deployment of nuclear weapons. Should launchers and other emplacements also be specifically forbidden within the agreed territory? It would seem so.

(2) The Underwriting of Nuclear-free Zones by the Nuclear Powers

Naturally, nuclear-free zones offer but the sparsest imitation of security if they are not recognised by the existing nuclear powers and if those powers do not give solemn undertakings to respect their status.

In the case of the Treaty of Tlatelolco, there are two protocols which have been endorsed by the nuclear powers, respecting and accepting the agreement that nuclear weapons may not be deployed within the Treaty area. The second protocol, for instance, agrees to fully respect the Treaty, and to refrain from violating it. It further commits its signatories not to use or threaten to use nuclear weapons against the contracting parties of the main Treaty.

Many people have questioned whether the Latin American Treaty goes far enough in the requirements it imposes on the nuclear powers. Should not those powers agree to prohibit the sale of nuclear materials which could be used for military purposes? Should they not agree to disconnect any linkages with nuclear weapons aspects of any existing military alliances? But undoubtedly the major problem about nuclear power recognition of nuclear-free zones is that of enforcement. To this we shall return later.

(3) The Development of a Nuclear-free Zone in Europe

The two sub-regions of Europe which have made most progress towards the development of nuclear-free zones are the Northern (Nordic) area and the Balkan zone. A recent conference in Athens brought together representatives from Romania, Bulgaria, Yugoslavia and Turkey, at the invitation of the Greek Government which hosted the meeting. Interestingly, there was a parallel conference involving some of the peace movements of Europe. Although this failed to agree a communique, it afforded useful opportunities for discussion. The Russell Foundation was denied admission, but we welcome the fact that the gathering was convened, and that the Greek authorities played so prominent a part in it.

The conference was preceded by a joint appeal against the deployment of nuclear missiles in Europe, launched by President Ceausescu of Romania and Andreas Papandreou, the Greek Prime Minister. In a courageous letter to Presidents Reagan and Andropov the two European statesmen opposed the deployment of intermediate range nuclear missiles in Europe, to the considerable annoyance of some client states such as Great Britain. (The Greek

Ambassador in London was informed by the Foreign Office that it was "extremely annoyed" that Greece had failed to consult Britain before joining in so unusual a declaration.)

The Athens conference began after a two week delay, whilst the Turkish Government manoeuvred about whether to join or not. The Romanians in particular reasonably insisted that a Balkan meeting needed Turkish representation, although the Turks were, at best, lukewarm about the proposal. From the beginning they made it clear that they did not believe that the Balkans could be separated from the rest of Europe on matters of nuclear weapons. However, they were anxious to be present in any multilateral gathering of Balkan states, and they agreed to attend provided the de-nuclearisation plan was placed last on an agenda of five points. Surprisingly, very prompt agreement was reached among the other states to accept this proviso. However, the Turks were not mollified by this, and when the talks took place, they maintained the unconstructive view that "the right forum for discussing nuclear weapons' control is the US-Soviet talks in Geneva, not somewhere on the periphery". Since the forum in question has collapsed, most people are hopeful that the periphery may prove more sensitive to disarmament needs than the alleged "centre" has shown itself. Greece and Turkey are the only Balkan nations harbouring nuclear weapons, so clearly it is necessary to try to secure Turkish agreement to the creation of a nuclear-free zone. Paradoxically, both Greece and Turkey are harbouring American nuclear weapons, even though mutual suspicions ensure the most uneasy of relationships between them. It is arguable that the conflict between Greece and Turkey is perhaps the most intransigent of all the national rivalries on the European mainland, and it is instructive that this fracture exists *within* one of the alliances, not across the divide of the cold war.

The commitment of the Greeks to a nuclear-free zone is evident, and is made plain in the fact that it was their initiative to convene the February 1984 conference. Bulgaria and Romania have also declared in favour of a nuclear-free zone, as has Yugoslavia. However, the Yugoslavs could reasonably insist that such a zone, constituted in a region so sensitive to superpower confrontations, would be meaningless without fully adequate guarantees from the United States and the Soviet Union. The Athens diplomatic conference ended with a cautious statement, promising to continue discussions.

The problem of securing compliance from the superpowers is, of course, to put it very mildly, no less intractable than that of reconciling the conflicting interests of Greece and Turkey. The United States has expressed strong opposition to the Balkan nuclear-free zone on the grounds that it would alter the strategic balances in the Eastern Mediterranean, without securing adequate concessions from the Soviet Union. The claim is that Warsaw Treaty armed forces are superior in conventional weaponry and that the Turkish and Greek nuclear weapons provide a necessary rung in the scale of "deterrent" forces. Many of us have argued against this point of view elsewhere, and it is hardly necessary to repeat those arguments here.

More seriously, since the deployment of Soviet intermediate range missiles in the German Democratic Republic and Czechoslovakia, it is argued by some independent scholars as well as Western specialists that the "neutralisation" of South Eastern Europe disproportionately weakens NATO's Southern flank. If the American presence were to be reduced or removed from this zone, such people have argued that Soviet pressures could easily increase, not only on Greece and Turkey, but also on Yugoslavia. Clearly, the reciprocal Central European deployments have hindered progress in the Balkans.

The heightened nuclear face-off between the two Germanies and in Central Europe has also been an undoubted set-back to the progress of the Nordic nuclear-free zone.

By contrast with the Balkan area, none of the Nordic states harbours nuclear weapons, and all have signed the non-proliferation treaty. Finland and Sweden are committed neutrals, and the Swedes have a consistent policy of "non-alignment in peace aiming at neutrality in war". Denmark, Norway and Iceland are aligned in NATO, but both the Danes and the Norwegians have declared that they will not allow nuclear weapons to be stationed on their territories during peacetime. In one sense, then, there is already an embryonic nuclear-free zone in Northern Europe. However, the separate commitments of the different states of the region do not have the benefit of underpinning by reciprocal commitments on the part of the nuclear powers. The quickest progress towards this would probably come from the formal conclusion of a treaty in the area which would leave nuclear powers caught in the crossfire of world public opinion.

Within the language of "mutual and balanced force reductions", it would be impossible for either superpower to justify heightened escalation in the central zone of Europe whilst both were moving to disengagement in the North and South. But it will not, long term, be sufficient for one superpower to sponsor the proposed lesser nuclear-free zones and underwrite them alone. This fact will be a brake on development unless there arises a real possibility of loosening up within one or another, if not both, alliance systems. For this reason, the campaign against the deployment of intermediate-range missiles across Europe retains a vital importance. From the point of view of the peace movements, to be sure, the triumph of a small nuclear-free zone on any sector of the dividing line between the blocs would be an important breakthrough. It is increasingly difficult to see any likely circumstances in which a single agreement could embrace the whole of Europe at one sweep: all the tangible progress towards discussion between Governments has so far taken place on a much smaller scale. Yet, even if the sometimes large obstacles to practical agreement in either the Balkan or Nordic regions could all be overcome there would remain a vast problem for the realisation of a comprehensive European solution. Smaller nuclear-free zones will meet with the same difficulties as larger ones, and foremost amongst these is the question of enforcement.

(4) Enforcement

The enforcement of a nuclear-free zone may not be easy for the individual consenting states within it. It is presumably possible for them to reach agreement about their own conduct, and any mechanisms for inspection and control which may be necessary. There exists an international body which is charged with controlling nuclear materials: the International Atomic Energy Agency. This Agency does not command universal support, and has been open to various criticisms. There seems to be no special reason why the IAEA should be the monopoly custodian of inspectors' powers within nuclear-free zones. The Treaty of Tlatelolco has an enforcement committee. It would be possible for new treaties to agree open inspection mechanisms which were as rigorous as their consenting parties felt to be desirable. However, whilst internal inspection by agreement is simple in principle, enforcement by observance on the outside nuclear powers is far more difficult. When nuclear powers feel their interests to be in jeopardy, they have already shown themselves to be less than scrupulous about the observance of international treaties. None of the wars which have plagued humanity during this century would have been possible if all the powers involved in them had respected all the treaty undertakings they had ever signed. More: there is even some evidence that the specific treaty establishing the nuclear-free zone in Latin America has already been violated by one, possibly by two existing nuclear powers.

During the conflict over the Falkland/Malvinas Islands, the British Government sent its fleet to the South Atlantic in order to recover control over these territories. This fleet was apparently not divested of its large arsenals of nuclear depth charges and other weapons. Indeed, there is a good deal of evidence that it would have been impossible so to have divested it, since its "deterrent" capacity, *vis à vis* the Soviet Union would have been completely negated for the duration of the war with Argentina, had this been done. Be that as it may, the Falkland flag ship has subsequently been compelled to limp around 'he Pacific, as it has been denied admission to ports in both Australia and Japan, on the grounds that it has a stock of nuclear weapons, which are forbidden in those areas. If the Australian Government, which is a key member of the British Commonwealth, feels that it has sufficient evidence to prohibit the dry-docking of this ship, this must seem a *prima facie* reason for suspecting a serious breach of the Treaty of Tlatelolco during the Falklands war.

In a similar sense, the presence of the American fleet off Nicaragua, in a large-scale deployment covering both the Pacific and Atlantic coasts of that country, also raises the fear that the United States may not be honouring its Treaty obligations.

Of course, both major powers frequently send their fleets into places where they are not entirely welcome. There have been repeated encroachments by Soviet submarines into Swedish territorial waters, for instance. But the breach of a nuclear-free zone agreement should surely be seen as a far more serious dereliction than simple trespass. That apparent violations of the Tlatelolco Treaty can pass with so little public comment is, perhaps, the chief weakness of the nuclear-free zone strategy of peace movements and non-aligned states. Unless we can mobilise effective and damaging public criticism of any and all violations, we shall not succeed in sanitising any great area of the world for any material length of time.

(5) The Role of the Peace Movement in Furthering Disarmament
If these arguments are justified, the enforcement of nuclear-free zones is only partly a matter for their member states. Of course, adequate inspection and technical control is extremely important, and mechanisms for imposing high standards remain to be achieved. There is much diplomatic work to do, in order to develop

the Latin American prototype of a nuclear-free zone so that it could operate in more contentious regions. But what happens when inspection reveals that it is a nuclear power which is acting in violation of non-nuclear agreements? The latest evidence on this score is provided in a related sphere: the United States' Government is credibly accused of mining Nicaraguan territorial waters, and causing damage both to Soviet and Japanese ships, amongst others. Clamorous evidence is offered by American politicians to the effect that mines have been directly placed by the Central Intelligence Agency. The refusal of the United States' Government to answer Nicaraguan complaints to the World Court, and its declared intention of ignoring any relevant proceedings of that Court for a period of two years, show us some of the limits of international law, when we confront such crucial issues as nuclear disarmament. How may the weak compel the strong? It seems transparently plain that institutions for reaching public opinion are more important than institutions of force, if this task is not to be rendered totally futile.

Links between peace movements have been the first stage in diagnosing this problem. Already the Japanese Council Against A and H Bombs has pioneered international contact on the widest scale and reached out to form links with the growing campaign for European Nuclear Disarmament.

In Europe, two successive Conventions of the main peace movements in Western and neutral states have established a continuing dialogue between the main organisations in the field. The first Convention, in Brussels, in 1982, was fortunate in having the presence of the Venerable Gyotsu Sato, who established close contacts with many of the most important organisations. Strong European representation resulted at the World Conference Against A and H Bombs in Tokyo in 1982, and again in 1983. A powerful delegation from Japan also attended the second European Nuclear Disarmament Convention which was held in Berlin in 1983. The growth of these contacts is of extraordinary importance. More and more American peace movements are relating to the initiatives of both European and Pacific peace activists. If there is one further task which now presses all of us, I think it is this: in a number of continental areas, the debate on the threat of nuclear war lags far behind the level already reached in the European and Pacific "theatres". I think that together, we should seek to consider how to encourage that debate, and how to widen the circle of contacts, so that the peace movement begins to create a veritable unity of all the peoples, able to defend all real steps towards disarmament, and to oppose any regression, no matter by whom. The forums of peace movements, both in the Pacific and in Europe, understand the need for a policy of strict non-alignment. Paradoxically, peace movements are less organised and less extensive in many of the areas where the movement of non-aligned states is strongest. Generally it is these states which suffer most from the bad behaviour of nuclear powers. Somehow, surely we must find a way to join our forces to this question.

This text was prepared for the International Conference against International Bases and Blocs, Okinawa, April 1984. I append an exchange of letters with the United Nations, which throws light on some of the questions it discusses.

Exchange of Letters

Mr Javier Perez de Cuellar, Secretary-General, United Nations, New York, USA, 3 June 1983.

Dear Secretary-General,
For some time now British public opinion has been disturbed by questions about the conduct of the Falklands War, and in particular by a serious controversy about the sinking of the Argentinian cruiser *Belgrano*.

The charges against Mrs Thatcher have been tersely summarised in an "information sheeet" (number 11) published by *Ecoropa* under the title *Falklands War: The Disturbing Truth*. There are two main counts in this indictment:

1. The cruiser *Belgrano* was sunk "so as to make peace impossible" even while an agreement for Argentine withdrawal from the islands was reaching its final stages.
2. That nuclear weapons were taken to the South Atlantic.

These matters are very grave and they surely merit a special enquiry in Britain. I shall certainly give all support to the demand for this enquiry if I am elected to the House of Commons on June 9th.

But these matters do not only affect the people of the United Kingdom. Both raise profound international questions.

The first charge, of sabotaging peace talks by sinking the *Belgrano,* amounts to an accusation that Mrs Thatcher or her agents breached the Nuremburg Principles of 1946, which provide the most authoritative summary of the decisions of the post-war War Crimes Tribunal. This Tribunal received unanimous endorsement for its findings at the General Assembly of the United Nations (see Resolution 95-i). The precise infraction alleged against Mrs Thatcher or her agents is covered in Principle VI as a 'crime against peace', qualified in Article a(i) as 'planning, preparation, initiation or waging a war . . . in violation of international . . . agreements or assurances'. It will be remembered that UN Resolution 502 demanded 'immediate cessation of hostilities' and withdrawal of Argentine forces, and called for a "diplomatic solution" respecting the UN Charter.

The second charge of sending nuclear weapons into the war zone, alleges a direct breach of the terms of the Treaty of Tlatelolco, under which Britain recognises the status of Latin America as a nuclear-free zone.

Can you advise us about how these issues could be properly investigated? We are particularly concerned about the enforcement of the Treaty of Tlatelolco, since we have been active in encouraging the proposal to create a nuclear-free zone in Europe. Clearly, the possible breach of the Latin American nuclear-free zone raises major questions. Disregard of nuclear-free zone arrangements would, if it were to go unopposed, totally negate the intentions of the UN Special Session on Disarmament, which commended such zones as an important confidence building measure.

At the same time, the legal implications of the sinking of the *Belgrano* are also deeply serious. There would be no "crime against peace" if there had been no UN Resolution 502, and if diplomatic approaches had been spurned on all or either sides. The armed forces on both sides were in no position to know about the extent of diplomatic progress. It is unlikely that the diplomats could expect to have detailed knowledge about military dispositions. Only at the point where decisions could be taken, weighing together both diplomatic and military issues, is there any possibility of a "crime against peace". For this reason, it seems to me that the United Nations is the only relevant body to investigate this issue.

With great respect,

Yours sincerely,

Ken Coates

United Nations, New York   26 August 1983

Dear Mr Coates,

I should like to refer to your letter of 3 June 1983, addressed to the Secretary General concerning certain matters pertaining to the conduct of the Falklands War.

We have carefully analysed the two issues you have raised in your letter which are of undoubted importance. The alleged introduction of nuclear weapons into the South Atlantic zone has been the object of a resolution by the General Conference of the Organisation for the Prohibition of Nuclear Weapons in Latin America (we are attaching a copy in Spanish, the only language available at this time). This Organisation might in fact be competent also to initiate an investigation on this matter.

As far as the United Nations is concerned, any investigation would have to follow the adoption of a resolution by one of the two political organs of the Organisation already seized of the question of the Falklands (Malvinas), namely the General Assembly or the Security Council. Such resolution would have to be sponsored by one or more member states.

Yours sincerely,

Richard W. Wathen, *Principal Officer,*
Department of Political Affairs,
Trusteeship and Decolonisation.

ORGANISATION FOR THE PROHIBITION OF NUCLEAR ARMS IN LATIN AMERICA

GENERAL CONFERENCE
Eighth (Ordinary) Period of Sessions
Item 18 on the Agenda
KINGSTON, JAMAICA: 16-19 May 1983

CG/RES. 170 (VIII) 18 May 1983

Resolution 170 (VIII) — Reports of the introduction of nuclear arms by the United Kingdom of Great Britain and Northern Ireland in the zone and areas of the Islas Malvinas, Georgias Del Sur and Sandwich Del Sur.

The General Conference,

Considering that the governments signatory to the Treaty of Tlatelolco have categorically expressed their determination that nuclear energy be used in Latin America exclusively for peaceful purposes and, to this end, reaffirmed their sovereign decision to establish a military de-nuclearised zone in order to keep their territories free, forever, of nuclear armaments;

Considering that the Argentinian Republic has denounced at various international gatherings the presence of nuclear weaponry aboard vessels of the British naval forces which operated in areas within the geographical zone designated by Paragraph 2 of Article 4 of the Treaty in connection with the conflict in the Islas Malvinas (Falkland Islands) and the South Georgias and South Sandwich Islands, pointing out in the light of this event the significance of countries in possession of nuclear weapons engaging in operations in which nuclear energy is put to non-peaceful uses;

Considering that spokesmen for the government of the United Kingdom have on several occasions declared that it would be inconvenient, for reasons of national security, to abandon the established practice, observed by successive governments, of neither confirming nor denying the presence or absence of nuclear weapons at a specific place and a given time;

Considering that the United Kingdom of Great Britain and Northern Ireland has made the declaration which appears in the document S/Inf. 261 of 11 May 1983;

Having regard to the fact that the Organisation for the Prohibition of Nuclear Arms in Latin America (OPANAL) has a duty to supervise compliance with the obligations laid down by the Treaty of Tlatelolco;

Reaffirming the need for a balance of responsibilities and obligations affecting states which possess nuclear arms and those which do not possess them;

Resolves:

1. *To note with concern* the complaint formulated by the Argentinian Republic concerning the introduction of nuclear arms, by the United Kingdom of Great Britain and Northern Ireland, into areas included in the geographical zone designated in Paragraph 2 of Article 4 of the Treaty of Tlatelolco.

2. *To take note* of the declaration by the United Kingdom of Great Britain and Northern Ireland to which the fourth Considering paragraph of this Resolution refers, and which states in its

leading paragraphs: "The Government of the United Kingdom has scrupulously complied with its obligations under Additional Protocol I to the Treaty for the Prohibition of Nuclear Arms in Latin America and has not deployed nuclear weapons in areas for which, *de jure* or *de facto,* it is internationally responsible and which are located within the limits of the geographical zone established in the said Treaty. Moreover, the Government has scrupulously complied with its obligations under Additional Protocol II to the Treaty and has not deployed nuclear weapons in areas where the Treaty is in force".

3. *To take note* of the important presentations and declarations formulated by the Delegations of Argentina and the United Kingdom at this General Conference.

4. *To express its concern* at the fact that in areas within the geographical zone designated by Paragraph 2 of Article 4 of the Treaty, submarines powered by nuclear energy should have been employed in warlike actions.

5. *To exhort* all States in respect of which the Treaty and its Additional Protocols are not in force, to take the necessary steps in accordance with Article 28 to complete the process of military de-nuclearisation in the relevant zone defined by Paragraph 2 of Article 4 of the Treaty itself.

6. *To reaffirm* the commitment of all States linked by the Treaty of Tlatelolco and its Additional Protocols, to refrain from carrying out all actions which might endanger the status of military de-nuclearisation of Latin America and to recommend that the Council of the Organisation closely supervise its strict enforcement.

7. *To communicate* to the General Assembly of the United Nations in its 38th Period of Sessions, and to the Disarmament Committee, the text of the present Resolution, together with the declarations made on the subject in the course of this Conference.

(Approved in the Forty-ninth Session, held on 19 May 1983).

Translated from the Spanish by Mike Mullan.

CHAPTER FOUR

Nuclear-free Zones in Britain

With the rebirth of the movement for nuclear disarmament in Britain, there has been a growing tendency for local and municipal councils to identify themselves with the cause by a simple but dramatic expedient. They approve resolutions declaring their area to be a nuclear-free zone. Beginning with an initiative in Manchester, this movement has now reached out to involve more than 100 other municipalities, including absolutely crucial bodies like the Greater London Council, and several major county authorities. As the number of nuclear-free authorities increased, it became necessary for them to liaise with one another, and their representatives gathered in Manchester on 21 October 1981 in order to discuss the problems which have arisen in implementing their decisions, and the scope for public education on the nuclear menace.

British local authorities are subject to detailed responsibilities within the framework of wartime emergency plans, codified under the Civil Defence (Planning) Regulations. Broadly, the large county authorities are required to draw up their own plans to deal with war dislocations and the smaller district councils are required to give support to this broader planning. The object of this planning was determined in the Civil Defence Act 1948, which required the Greater London Council and all the county councils of England and Wales to "make plans for providing and maintaining a range of local services essential to the life of the local community in the event of an hostile attack". The later regulations lay down duties for the smaller district councils and the London Borough Councils: they must provide information for civil defence purposes to the defence planning units above them, and they must assist their county authorities in drawing up such plans. The Home Office, for instance, sent a circular in January 1974, requesting all these district authorities "to increase their effort" in order to select and

*Parts of this text appeared in *ENDpapers 2* (Spokesman, 1982).

◀ *Bradford Town Hall.*

prepare local authority premises which could be used as headquarters in wartime; to detail adequate planning staffs to cope with such emergencies; to co-ordinate planning of fire services; to improve community involvement in civil defence, using more volunteers; and to search out suitable nuclear shelters which could be opened to the public.

The scope of the county war plans themselves is rather more sinister. It is assumed that in the event of nuclear war people who live in the devastated areas will try to leave, and will have to be prevented from doing so. It is assumed that the sick will be untreatable and that the main public health activity will be the disposal of corpses. The horrendous problems of administering martial law in a society which is literally disintegrating can be glimpsed in these county documents, which is why they have been kept secret over many years, only beginning to emerge in public as a result of disaffection among local government staff shocked by the implications of such policies. It is of course assumed that the police will speedily arrest all disaffected people, around whom oppositions might cohere. It is further assumed that there would be need for absolute control over all motor transport, telephone communications, and public information. In short, the county war plans lay down a detailed blueprint for the establishment of a complete dictatorship, ruling by naked force, unmediated by any democratic sanction.

Working within this framework, the most bizarre suggestions can be seriously discussed. At one police briefing which was conducted under the influence of these plans, a senior officer seriously suggested that swimming pools should be sealed off from the public, because it would be possible to fill them with brine in order to pickle cadavers, which would make "a valuable source of protein".

Small wonder that the civil defence powers are shrouded in official secrecy. Few local authority officials will talk with the press about their emergency planning departments. The relevant committees do not normally publish minutes and most councillors are not aware of what goes on in them. When councillors have to be briefed by the officials, they are usually warned that the Official Secrets Act applies to the information about to be transmitted.

On 12 May 1982 the following letter was sent from the Home Office to the Chief Executives of all the county councils in England and Wales:

Dear Sir,

Exercise Hard Rock

The Home Office, in conjunction with the United Kingdom Commanders in Chief Committees, have started preparations for a major home defence exercise "Hard Rock" lasting for two or three days in October 1982. The exercise is at present only at an outline planning stage but it will be broadly on the lines of Exercise "Square Leg", based on a nuclear attack with play in the post attack period. Planning will assume greater civil participation than in "Square Leg". It is our aim to have in all sub-regional headquarters the designated Principal and Deputy Principal Officers, representatives of the Home Office, other Government Departments and the emergency services, scientific advisers and the Military Advisory Teams. Full benefit from the exercise will depend upon comparable civil teams at county and district levels.

No central government funds additional to those referred to in Home Office Circular ES 1/1981 can be allocated for the exercise. The duration and extent of participation is at the discretion of local authorities and chief constables. It is, however, hoped that the additional funds now available towards training expenses as a result of the home defence review will assist local authorities to play a full part in an exercise designed to offer opportunities for extensive civil involvement.

I should be glad if you would let me know by 31 May if in principle you would be prepared for your authority to take part in this exercise. Further particulars will be announced as soon as possible.

I am sending copies of this letter to Secretaries of the Association of County Councils and the Association of Metropolitan Authorities for their information.

Yours faithfully,

J.A. Howard

Exercise "Hard Rock" was reported in the Sheffield *Morning Telegraph* in September 1981, and the chairman of the South Yorkshire County Council's anti-nuclear working party immediately made a public statement that he had never been informed of this operation. Soon it became clear that not only South Yorkshire but also the adjacent Labour controlled authorities of Derbyshire and Nottinghamshire, all of which have declared themselves to be nuclear-free zones, had been hooked into the Home Office scheme by their senior full-time officials, who had simply not informed their councillors, for all the fact that they were legally responsible for such decisions.

The national policy of the Labour Party on civil defence insists that none of the Government's proposed measures provide any genuine protection for the people of Britain, if there is a nuclear war. Accordingly, they are a waste of money which can only have one rational purpose, that of fraudulently persuading people that they are "secure" when security is impossible. However, the Labour Party acknowledges that while "civil" defence (the protection of the civil population from the effects of nuclear war) does not exist in Britain, the Government is energetically concerned with what it calls "Home Defence". This is expensively designed in order to preserve a tiny elite corps of Government and military personnel. The Labour Party protest at "the fact that the civilian population is told to stay home and that essential supplies and all major communications routes are to be reserved for the military, means that the Government anticipates the death of a very high proportion of the population living in cities or in rural areas near military bases, communications centres and other targets".

In this realisation, the National Executive of the Labour Party recommended local authorities to expose the use of "civil" defence as a brain-washing mechanism, calculated to generate the myth that it is possible to survive a nuclear war. The NEC recommended local authorities to "adopt" a policy of opposition to nuclear weapons being manufactured, deployed or positioned within the boundaries of the local authority. The Labour Party also advised its local councillors to discard the war planning role of emergency planning officers, only maintaining plans for peace time disasters; and it suggested that local authorities should reject co-operation with "all but the bare legal minimum necessary under the 1974 Civil Defence (Planning) Regulations". Labour authorities "should not participate in emergency planning exercises and arrangements which are concerned with nuclear weapons and nuclear preparations". At the same time, the Labour Party recommended that local authorities should seek to do everything possible to encourage public education on the dangers and effects of nuclear war.

The initial resolution passed by the Manchester City Council read as follows:

"Manufacture and Deployment of Nuclear Weapons

Resolution passed by Manchester City Council

This Council, in the light of its predetermined policy concerning the dangers of nuclear weapons, calls upon Her Majesty's Government to refrain from the manufacture or positioning of any nuclear weapons of any kind within the boundaries of our city.

Conscious of the magnitude of the destructive capacity of modern nuclear weapons, we recognise that our proposals would have little meaning on their own. We therefore directly appeal to our neighbouring authorities in the North West of England and to all local authorities throughout Great Britain to make similar statements on behalf of the citizens they represent.

We believe that it is not in the interests of our people to be either the initiators or the magnet of a nuclear holocaust and firmly believe that such unequivocal statements would clearly indicate the overwhelming desires of the people we represent and could lay the groundwork for the creation and development of a nuclear-free zone in Europe''.

Some 75 local authorities joined with Manchester at their conference on 21 October 1981. 165 Delegates were present, and it was reported that the total number of local authorities now aligned with the Manchester initiative was 123. In the 10 days following the conference, a further six authorities added their support.

The Manchester conference established a steering committee, representing each different type of local authority in England, Scotland and Wales. The Manchester authority was asked to provide the secretary of this committee, which had the following terms of reference:

1. To consider what initiatives should be taken by local authorities, acting together, to further the aim of reducing the possibilities of nuclear conflict, including contacts with other countries;
2. To examine the powers and duties of local authorities in relation to Civil Defence Planning and associated matters;
3. To seek detailed Counsel's opinion on the question and in the light of such information to consider how the proposed initiatives can be reconciled with statutory powers and duties; also what changes in the law should be demanded.

The steering committee would also compare notes about the question of possible related action concerning the uses of nuclear energy and the problems of nuclear waste. These problems have been increased since the decision to refine Japanese nuclear waste in Great Britain, presumably in order to recover militarily useful plutonium.

After careful consideration the councils which were to join the new steering committee were agreed: they were, Avon County Council, Dumbarton District Council, Greater London Council, Gwent County Council, Islington London Borough Council, Leicester City Council, Lothian Regional Council, Sheffield City Council, Tyne and Wear County Council, and Wrexham Maelor District Council.

The work of the steering committee will almost certainly produce rallying points at which the local government machinery of Great

Britain will be able to exert strong pressure for legislative reform. Meantime, a list of the activities undertaken by councils, is quite impressive. In Manchester, peace organisations have been given free use of premises and facilities; space has been devoted to the problem of nuclear war in the civic newspaper; exhibitions have been displayed in the public libraries; market stalls have been made available to peace activists; a carnival against the missiles has been sponsored; a new park in the city has been given the name Peace Park; and discussions in local schools and meetings with professional teaching associations have considered the problems of peace studies. At the same time, Manchester has restricted attendance at the Home Defence College, and re-examined its responsibilities in relation to Governmental war plans. Manchester has also begun a work of international diplomacy on a grand scale. The Manchester resolution has been discussed at meetings in East and West Germany, France, Holland, Sweden, Denmark and Czechoslovakia. Councillor Risby represented Manchester at the Rome Conference, sponsored by the Russell Foundation, in order to organise the forthcoming European Nuclear Disarmament Convention.

The same kinds of activities have been promoted in all the other 128 authorities. Some have published special materials, while others have withdrawn misleading civil defence publications which had previously been circulated. The Sheffield City Council has discovered how to give grants to peace groups from the proceeds of local lotteries. The Bradford Metropolitan District Council has opened up the hitherto secret war bunker to local press and television, an exercise in municipal pedagogy which made a profound impact.

In July 1981, I wrote on behalf of the Russell Foundation to all the signatories of the European Nuclear Disarmament appeal, enclosing details of the Manchester initiative and the Labour Party's Civil Defence policies. Numerous Europeans who were interested in local government expressed interest, and as a direct result of this contact there is already a movement in Denmark for various cities to table their own nuclear-free zone proposals. In Italy, Bologna was the first city to publish the END appeal in the municipal journal, during the summer of 1980. Subsequently, the commune of Riccione has undertaken a major exercise along the same lines.

The device of town twinning is a natural grapevine through which this kind of reaction can be spread. It is to be hoped that

such organisations as the United Towns will be able to lend their
support to this process so that it can become a truly European
initiative.

Appendix

Derbyshire's Nuclear War Plan

The Derbyshire Times made the county's nuclear war plan its lead story
over two weeks in March 1981. The author of both reports is Ian Amos.

Anti-nuclear campaigners claim to have penetrated the secrecy
surrounding top level war planning in Derbyshire.

Members of a "ban-the-bomb" pressure group say they are now in
possession of restricted documents. Their information is said to have come
from within the county's war emergency department based at the County
Office in Matlock.

Within the next few days, they intend to take the wraps off Derbyshire's
War Emergency Plan — detailing how the county would handle a nuclear
attack — the document which up to now has been guarded by secrecy.

But yesterday Derbyshire County Council warned the campaigners of the
consequences of releasing "sensitive" information.

The campaigners claim their action will unmask the futility behind the
war plan, and will reveal how "totally ineffective" the action suggested in
it will prove.

They are also planning to reveal information gathered during last year's
Derbyshire involvement with a national war exercise known as "Operation
Square Leg".

The group claiming to have breached security is known as Matlock
Against Nuclear Arms (MANA) and has become increasingly prominent in
its base town since forming last year.

From a nucleus of a few committed locals, deeply concerned with the
arms race, the group has built up a membership of more than 100 and has
contact with the CND organisation.

Revealing the decision to unveil Derbyshire's war plan and to release
local details of "Operation Square Leg", the group says: "Both have been
shrouded in secrecy, but MANA believes that in a democracy people have a
right to know what is being planned on their behalf — particularly when it
involves the death of millions of ordinary British citizens".

They say there is an "horrifying banality" about the war plan, and add:
The measures proposed would be totally ineffective in preventing the death
of the majority of the population and appalling suffering for the survivors
over an indefinite time . . ."

The Derbyshire War Plan — drawn up and reviewed over the past years
— is said to be a slim document. Each page is headed with the word
"Restricted", and only a handful of County Council officials and members
are issued with copies.

MANA claim to have a copy of "Part One" of the plan — the second
part is currently being drawn up.

The plan is said to detail exactly how the County Council would react to a war situation.

Information is given about:

How certain chief council officers, led by Derbyshire Chief Executive Mr Neil Ashcroft as controllers, would be deployed in an official "war team". .   .

How such a team would begin to cope with a complete communications breakdown, extensive damage and fires, lethal radiation levels, and thousands of people injured, homeless and hungry.

Where the officials and military staff would be located in bunkers. Already it is understood, such bunkers exist in Matlock and Derby under many feet of concrete.

How schools and community centres could be used as temporary hospitals and emergency feeding centres.

Where and how crucial food supplies could be stored.

MANA also claim to have details about Derbyshire's part in last year's "Operation Square Leg" exercise — information which they say came from "directly within the County Council's control room".

The details are said to cover the size and type of local areas hit by projected bomb blasts.

In the last exercise — say MANA — such areas included Derby city centre, and Sheffield, which would mean a fallout of radiation across the Chesterfield district.

References are also made to the controversial cruise missile bases planned within a hundred miles of Derbyshire.

All the details are due to be released at a public meeting next Friday.

One of the leading members of MANA, Mr Clive Newton of Winster, told me: "I think people want to know these things and they have a right to know. People are being conned into belief that nuclear war won't be as bad as it will be".

He added: "The message we want to get across is that by making Britain the main nuclear arsenal for Europe we're making it the main nuclear target in any war. If that's the case, then there's nothing civil defence can do to save the vast majority of the population, and those that are left will wish they had died".

Not wishing to reveal how MANA had gained its information, Mr Newton said: "People are not being given the facts. Now, we have a copy of the plan and we can show people that it is totally unrealistic".

Informed by the *Derbyshire Times* that an anti-nuclear group had possession of the war plans, Derbyshire Council issued the following statement:

"The County Council has responsibility to prepare plans to assist survival in the aftermath of war. Those plans in outline are not confidential. Some of the details, however, are classified by the Government as confidential because their disclosure could prejudice the effectiveness of measures intended to help protect the public.

"Therefore, any organisation intending to publish the full details of the county or district plans should consider the consequences carefully.

"In the even of war, local authorities have a duty to provide shelter and food for the surviving population. That is what the plans are for and any action which would impede those plans, such as a disclosure of sensitive information about communications systems, would be against the public interest.

"The County Council is always ready to discuss its role in this field and the emergency plans with any interested organisation or individuals. Press and broadcasting interviews on the subject have been given frequently and we do not wish to stifle public debate on the issues. However, in very limited areas some details must remain confidential and we're sure the good sense of this is understood."

13 March 1981

The wraps came off Derbyshire's "restricted" war plan this week, revealing a grim insight into the terrors of a nuclear aftermath.

The revelation was made by members of an anti-nuclear group who claim the secret plan would prove "futile" in the event of war.

To back their claims, the campaigners on Tuesday carried out their intention to unveil details of the plan — as revealed by the *Derbyshire Times* last week.

Those details, backed by other information from the recent war exercise known as "Operation Square Leg", and Government circulars, built up into a horror-catalogue of death, misery, disease and rioting.

The disclosures — which the campaigners say have been "shrouded in secrecy" up to now — included descriptions of how following a nuclear strike:

People selected as Controllers at County, District and Parish levels would be empowered to pass the death sentence when they thought fit.

People seriously injured and requiring treatment at special First Aid posts would be issued with coloured labels. A red label would mean treatment, and likely recovery would follow. But at the other end of the scale those bearing yellow labels would be asked to wait in special areas because they were expected to die anyway.

Road blocks would be set up during the build-up to a nuclear attack, preventing people attempting to leave heavily populated and therefore more vulnerable city areas. Any who did make their way to rural areas could be left to fend for themselves, the group claimed.

Food supplies would be commandeered from every home and then distributed on a one meal per person per day basis.

Home owners would be expected to take in "refugees" who had nowhere else to go. The plan was based on a basis of three refugees for every person already in a house. Outbuildings could also be taken over for that purpose.

People would be asked to form work-gangs to bury the dead and help in other areas. With radiation poisoning still a danger, they could be offered double rations as an incentive, the group added.

Cars would be confiscated, along with any fuel. No cooking would be allowed, and nobody would be allowed to make a phone call.

The group also gave detailed information about "Operation Square Leg" — the exercise where experts predict how a nuclear strike would affect the area.

They told how the recent exercise had covered the full build-up to war, including an evacuation of art treasures but not people, and the appearance of the Prime Minister on TV.

The group also described how Derbyshire's war control room — based in the County Offices at Matlock — would be put on alert:

> Strong advice against people leaving their homes would be given, and the film "Protect and Survive" would be shown.
>
> The alarm would be sounded by sirens from five police stations in the county, plus a further 280 hand-held sets in the rural areas.
>
> Under "Operation Square Leg", the group claimed, the first bomb landed within nine minutes. Sheffield city centre received a projected three megaton ground blast causing a 14-mile firestorm.
>
> Derby city centre was wiped out with a two megaton air blast, again causing extensive fires. Anyone standing 40 miles away from such an explosion would still receive second-degree burns, the group claimed.
>
> Forty-eight hours after such a strike, most of Britain would be covered by radioactive fallout 10 times higher than the lethal intensity.
>
> "Operation Square Leg" assumed 40 million died in Britain — but the campaigners claim the total would be greater.

Behind the war plan revelation is an organisation known as Matlock Against Nuclear Arms.

He went on to describe the pretence and secrecy of the Derbyshire war plans as "a con-trick on the public".

He questioned whether there would be the slow build-up to war predicted in "Square Leg", referring to the Cuba crisis when Governments held back for fear of inflaming the situation.

He doubted the reality of families spending at least two weeks in an "inner shelter" the size of a cupboard — as described in "Protect and Survive".

Mr Newton also questioned the reaction of people told to stay at home in a nuclear strike. He said: "You stay at home and die, or leave home and starve".

He also wondered what the reaction of rural people would be when they were asked to feed and house refugees. "Would people surviving be content with that? If they didn't want them, how strongly could they resist them? What are local residents going to think about thousands of refugees flooding into their villages and eating their food? Mr Newton asked.

Said Mr Newton: "Having outlined what's likely to happen it's obvious that there's no democracy at all. The war emergency plan suspends the democratic procedure".

MANA members are now calling on the County Council and local government to drop such plans and admit there is nothing they can do about nuclear war.

Mr Newton added, "Local authorities can refuse to enter into this type of planning and quite a few already have".

Told of the intended disclosures last week, the County Council said the group should bear in mind the consequences of revealing "sensitive" information.

Mr Newton said this week: "We don't think these things should be secret. We're not criticising Derbyshire's emergency planning department — we feel it's impossible to prepare a good plan. Local authorities should drop the pretence and secrecy".

20 March 1981

Reproduced by permission of the Derbyshire Times.

CHAPTER FIVE

Option for Nullity

At the time of writing*, President Reagan's statement on the so-called "zero option" is still awaited. But it is already apparent that the Geneva talks at the end of November 1981 are likely to to be dominated by this concept. Put at its crudest, the "zero gambit", as *The Times* more cynically styles it, involves an offer by the United States to end its planned deployment of Tomahawk Cruise and Pershing II missiles in Western Europe, provided the Soviet Union makes a "matching" bid, usually encapsulated in the West as a demand for the scrapping of the SS20 missiles. Thus, Denis Healey has told us that NATO's decision of December 1979

> "implied a readiness to abandon Pershing II and Cruise if Russia reduced her SS20s" (20 September 1981)

while Herr Genscher, four days later, said that there would be no need for the new medium range (presumably meaning "Long Range Theatre" in NATO jargon) nuclear forces

> "if the Soviet arms build-up is eliminated altogether."

Here we already have one source of difficulty in the "zero" proposals: they mean different things to different people on the same side of the argument. A large part of the Soviet military build-up is directed against China, but it is to say the least, implausible for NATO to seek to negotiate this. Socialists and pacifists, of course, all hope for the reciprocal disarmament in the Sino-Soviet confrontation, and for this reason resolutely oppose attempts in the West to "play the China card". But Soviet negotiators are unlikely to prove flexible about their Chinese frontiers until this detente has begun, and it is unlikely to open before there have been big changes in the Soviet leadership itself. If, on the other hand, as Mr Healey seems to think, the "zero" proposals refer to Euro-strategic

---

*This article was written for *Pace e Guerra* a few days before President Reagan revealed his proposals for a "zero option". Widely leaked, these proposals provoked considerable commentary even before they were officially published.

Greenham Common.

weapons only, then they raise a very large number of specific problems.

First among these is the framework of NATO policy itself. The original decision to go ahead with the territorially based Cruise and Pershing II systems was not all founded on the threat of the SS20, but on their suitability to bridge an alleged gap in the structure of "flexible response". Flexible response is polite NATO language for the doctrine of limited nuclear war. The new missiles were designed to provide new rungs in a ladder of escalation, and were thus situated within the framework of NATO's existing armament, to fit its own priorities rather than respond to others.

I should be clear about this. From the beginning the Russell Foundation has opposed the deployment of Soviet SS20s, which have a range restricted to the European theatre, and which clearly threaten all the peoples of our continent. But, as the apologists for Soviet military policy have always claimed, (and on this one matter they are not wrong) the SS20 replaces earlier more inaccurate but more powerful systems which were similarly deployed and targeted, and were arguably an even bigger threat to European survival, if such can be imagined. Unlike the apologists, we believe all these weapons, old and new, should be withdrawn and scrapped. It was in this spirit that the original appeal for European Nuclear Disarmament opposed the SS20 as well as the new generation of NATO missiles. But we have never accepted the argument that justifies the armament on one side simply by invoking that on another. That is the justification of the arms race, and it is the arms race itself which is the fundamental threat that must be reversed. As the Italian communists have argued, if "parities" are sought, they should be approached by disarming downwards to lower levels, not by arming upwards to higher ones. Of course the difficulty is that this reasonable proposal is always thwarted by the insuperable problem of comparing the impact of different systems. And this problem arises because the arms race is an insane game of leapfrog, in which ever-newer, even more diverse weapons are fielded in order to combat yesterday's innovations. Thus, NATO decides to spend millions on developing intelligent munitions to counter Soviet tank forces. This implies a decision not to concentrate expenditure on tanks, and equally implies an "imbalance" in tanks. But how do we equate numbers of tanks with numbers of "smart" anti-tank missiles? No-one tries. Instead, once one new technology is applied, another is developed to supersede it, and the apparent tank imbalance is invoked to "justify" the neutron bomb. In such difficulties a long succession of arms control initiatives have foundered. The SALT II talks laboured for seven years, only to produce an agreement which has not only not been implemented, but which has been followed by the decision in the United States to go ahead with installing the awesome MX system of intercontinental missiles.

All the evidence is that the zero option will involve talks of similar length. They will also involve similar failure, if the European mass-movement relaxes its pressure. The December 1979 NATO decision involved a notional "two track" commitment to deployment and negotiation. The West would put in the missiles while it bargained about them. In the context of preparation for limited nuclear war, the track of negotiation was necessary to cover the deservedly more unpopular track of deployment. The rise of the peace movement has forced governments to offer the hint that this process can be reversed, so that deployment can provide an incentive to agreement in the talks. This hint absolutely requires a response of deep suspicion. Deployment will go ahead, with consequences which could be irreversible, if we do not insist on the alternative.

And there is only one alternative to limited nuclear war in Europe, which is European Nuclear Disarmament. This is the only genuine option for peace. It insists upon the removal of all warheads from our continent, and the realisation of an agreement based upon the protocol of the United Nations Special Session on Disarmament, concerning the establishment of nuclear-weapons-free-zones. Such zones in Europe, which may well begin by embracing sub-regions like the Baltic, the Balkans, Iberia or the Mediterranean, will be the subject of negotiated agreements with the nuclear powers, guaranteeing their inviolability in treaties at least as comprehensive as that of Tlatelolco, governing the Latin American continent. (It is, of course, highly possible that this first example of a nuclear-free zone in a populous area can be improved upon.) When Europe rejects the scenario of limited war, the forces which keep the blocs apart will begin to melt away. At the same time, because the superpowers will then face the clear threat that the forces of each are henceforward predominently targeted upon the other, they will begin to take global disarmament seriously. Any lesser step that this is not really a zero option, it is an option for nullity.

If anyone doubts this, let her or him examine the likely results of the zero option on actual military policy. Supposing all the new

NATO missiles were to be taken off our landmass, and deployed from the sea. Would that make us safer? It is profoundly doubtful. Some of us would be even less safe. Supposing all the SS20s and the Euro-strategic weapons were removed from European Russia, which was then attacked from the North Sea or the Mediterranean. Can we imagine that Oslo or Rome would then escape destruction from the long-range Soviet missiles which would remain unaffected by such an agreement? Long-range missiles can shoot short, and if the awful spectre of limited war is not exorcised, they very probably will.

For these most potent reasons, the peace movement must remain active before, during and after the Geneva talks. We must refuse hospitality to the new missiles, and we must reject limited war. In this way we must insist on a continental withdrawal from the race to nuclear extinction. And we must get together, all of us, East and West, to insist upon our common future over and beyond the option for nullity.

CHAPTER SIX

Sakharov and the Bomb: Two Letters

In July 1981 Mrs Eileen Bernal, the widow of the famous scientist and herself a veteran campaigner for disarmament, circulated a letter she had addressed to Academician Sakharov. This raised several questions which deserved a reply. Both her original letter and my reply are featured below.

10 July 1981

Dear Professor Sakharov,
I take the liberty of writing to you partly because of the regard in which my late husband, Professor J.D. Bernal, held your scientific work (I believe he met you in the '50s), but also because I have received a copy of the letter you sent to Professor Alexandrov, President of the Soviet Academy of Sciences, in October 1980.

Naturally I cannot speak on Professor Bernal's behalf, but I have consulted with a few of his close colleagues, and they agree he would probably have endorsed the contents of this letter.

I find it difficult to reconcile what seem to be contradictory statements in your letter to Professor Alexandrov: on the one hand you are "convinced that the prevention of the thermo-nuclear war threatening mankind is our most important problem, having absolute priority over all other problems" and that "Disarmament, in particular nuclear disarmament, is mankind's most important task". Please believe me that these convictions of yours are sincerely shared by the entire peace movement in my country; we are dedicated to carrying out their realisation along with the peace movements of other countries, including the Soviet Union and the United States.

As you will know, the scientists' Pugwash Movement, the World Peace Council, the World Council of Churches, the World Disarmament Campaign, the organisations of Parliamentarians, of Women, Youth and many others, are linked together over the globe

◀ *Academician Sakharov.*

in working for these vital principles which have been so clearly summed up in the UN Final Document of the Special Session Devoted to Disarmament in 1978.

It is therefore tragic and contradictory to find that after you have stated your priorities, the major part of your letter to Professor Alexandrov is devoted to your "struggle for the observation of human rights and the rule of law". We too are involved in the question of human rights, but the ability to fight on this front — a front that has no consensus of definition as "rights" differ in different parts of the world — does depend on being *alive* to be able to do so. This brings us straight back to your priority, the right to life itself, freedom from the nuclear holocaust and the terrible awareness that man-made extinction of ourselves and our planet is less than 4½ minutes away. To substitute secondary and long-term reforms for the absolute necessity for life itself, and to trivialise the ghastly issues at stake by comparing censorship, alcoholism and the pollution of lakes to the mortal danger in which we stand, does not tally with that prior necessity which must determine our action. It is inconsistent.

I feel sure you must share the fear that scientists and non-scientists alike are filled with: that time is not on our side and that an accident or a mad finger on the trigger may quite easily launch us into infinity. It is not unlikely. This fear is darkening all our lives, and as you will know, the clock of the Atomic Scientists now stands at four minutes to midnight. Scientists everywhere are particularly fearful, being more acutely aware of the cataclysmic risks; but they realise, together with all peoples, that our only hope lies in the unifying efforts to resist, and they are "bonding" themselves together ever more broadly and tightly to meet this growing threat. It is therefore a contradiction in terms to find your name is not included among the famous American, British, Soviet, German and other scientists, who from Einstein and Russell to Joliot Curie, Feld, Bernal, Kistiakovsky, Feodorov, Burhop, have united their efforts to work world-wide to implement the Einstein & Russell Manifesto. In this Manifesto you will recollect the question is asked "Shall we . . . choose death because we cannot forget our quarrels?" I feel it must surely be regretted by the ever-growing body of scientists engaged in resisting the war danger that your negative answer means a real loss to their movement.

One cannot help asking why you have isolated yourself from the universal peace movement: never has there been a time when "One for all and all for one" is more needful for a successful outcome to our problems. You have some complaints against some of your colleagues, and the tenor of your letter to Professor Alexandrov is mainly accusatorial, but perhaps I may submit to you that in this imperfect world we are all of us at *some* time in our lives mistreated by *some* of our neighbours. Do you not feel at this moment in time the overriding priority must be life itself, that we are staring death in the face and that the only solution lies solely in the hands of the international peace movement?

Many of us join in hoping you will reconsider your position.

Yours sincerely,
Eileen Bernal

*   *   *

21 July 1981

Dear Mrs Bernal,

Thank you for sending a copy of your letter to Academician Sakharov.

What your late husband might have said about Academician Sakharov's letter to Professor Alexandrov I don't know, because unfortunately he is unable to tell us. I would like to think you might be mistaken. But just as you feel you can intuit his opinion, so also I know what Bertrand and Edith Russell would have said, and what would most likely have been the opinion of J.B.S. Haldane and other distinguished British scientists who worked hard for humane social advance. They would have paid respectful attention to Sakharov, partly because they were as a matter of principle concerned to defend the civil liberties of the common people in every country, and partly because they knew the penalties which official obscurantism can levy on free scientific enquiry. The official murder of Vavilov, and the rule of the charlatan Lysenko over Soviet genetics, cost the peoples of the Soviet Union a high price in forfeited material progress.

It is a truism to say that Sakharov needs to be alive in order to continue defending human rights. But you appear to be saying that his struggle against what any reasonable person must regard as intolerable persecution is in some metaphysical way opposed to that in which we are all engaged for nuclear disarmament and peace. This is a damaging and mistaken view, and it plays right into the hands of those extremists who tell us that civil freedoms in the USSR can only be advanced by escalating the cold war. The contrary is true. Detente and human rights taken together are a powerful solvent of those toxins which generate war psychoses. That the USSR unjustly penalises Sakharov harms the movement for peace in the Western countries, and reinforces the fear that the Soviet Union is opposed in principle to those democratic rights which you and I both value very highly for ourselves. This fear is only partly based on reality, and the conventional Western view is also shot through with self-serving mythology: but I am sure that you would agree that, if Sakharov were free to speak and to travel, and indeed to exercise those rights which were so fully and often courageously used by your late husband in propagating his ideas, (whether right, as was often the case, or wrong, as sometimes happened) then the USSR would instantly win over large sympathies among liberal-minded people in the West where today it provokes disquiet and apprehension.

What would you and I have said if Professor Bernal had been confined in a form of house arrest in mid-Wales, and subjected to the indignities which have been visited on Sakharov? What would he have said if Burhop, Haldane and Hogben had been put to hard labour for criticising the Government, while Russell was confined in an asylum and forcibly drugged? Beyond doubt we would have agreed that nuclear war was a worse evil than the repression visited upon our friends. But would we, for that reason, have asked them to suffer silently? You must know we could not have done so.

Personally, I do not agree with some of Sakharov's opinions. But on the topic you have chosen to raise with him, he has been a brave witness for truth. In his memoirs he describes his view of the resumption of Soviet nuclear tests in the atmosphere, in 1961:

"Beginning in 1957 (not without the influence of statements on this subject made throughout the world by such people as Albert Schweitzer, Linus Pauling, and others) I felt myself responsible for the problem of radioactive contamination from nuclear explosions. As is known, the absorption of the radioactive products of nuclear explosions by the billions of people inhabiting the earth leads to an increase in the incidence of several diseases and birth defects, of so-called sub-threshold biological effects — for example, because of damage to DNA molecules, the bearers of heredity. When the radioactive products of an explosion get in the atmosphere, each megaton of the nuclear explosion means thousands of unknown victims. And each series of tests of a nuclear weapon (whether they be conducted by the United States, the USSR, Great Britain, China, or France) involves tens of megatons; i.e. tens of thousands of victims.

In my attempts to explain this problem, I encountered great difficulties — and a reluctance to understand. I wrote memorandums (as a result of one of them I.V. Kurchatov made a trip to Yalta to meet with Khrushchev in an unsuccessful attempt to stop the 1958 tests), and I spoke at conferences. I remember that in the summer of 1961 there was a meeting between atomic scientists and the chairman of the Council of Ministers, Khrushchev. It turned out that we were to prepare for a series of tests that would bolster up the new policy of the USSR on the German question (the Berlin Wall). I wrote a note to Khrushchev, saying: 'To resume tests after a three-year moratorium would undermine the talks on banning tests and on disarmament, and would lead to a new round in the armaments race — especially in the sphere of intercontinental missiles and anti-missile defence'. I passed it up the line. Khrushchev put the note in his breast pocket and invited all present to dine. At the dinner table he made an off-the-cuff speech that I remember for its frankness, and that did not reflect merely his personal position. He said more or less the following: Sakharov is a good scientist. But leave it to us, who are specialists in this tricky business, to make foreign policy. Only force — only the disorientation of the enemy. We can't say aloud that we are carrying out our policy from a position of strength, but that's the way it must be. I would be a slob, and not Chairman of the Council of Ministers, if I listened to the likes of Sakharov. In 1960 we helped to elect Kennedy with our policy. But we don't give a damn about Kennedy if he is tied hand and foot — if he can be overthrown at any moment.''

Mr Khrushchev also in his own memoirs refers to this same episode:

"I used to meet frequently with Sakharov, and I considered him an extremely talented and impressive man. He was also a surprisingly young man to be involved in such important and difficult matters. He proposed that we develop a hydrogen bomb. No one else, neither the Americans nor the English, had such a bomb. I was overwhelmed by the idea. We did everything in our power to assure the rapid realisation of Sakharov's plans. With the help of engineers, technicians, and workers, our industry was able to develop the bomb in a remarkably short time. The hydrogen bomb represented a great contribution to the Soviet people and a great act of patriotism by Comrade Sakharov.

We later entered into negotiations with the United States and its allies on an agreement to halt the arms race. In the spirit of those negotiations, our side discontinued all nuclear explosions. Our scientists, of course, continued to work on the design of our weapons. They considerably reduced the cost and increased the power of a single explosion. But this was only on paper. Because we had voluntarily and unilaterally suspended our nuclear testing, there was no way our scientific and military experts could see if the new improved designs really worked.

Meanwhile during the many months that we suspended all tests, the Americans went right on testing, perfecting, and stockpiling their own bombs. We hoped that international public opinion would support us and exert pressure on the United States to stop contaminating the atmosphere, which people all over the world must breathe, but the American government was deaf to all protests. Thus, we were faced with the dilemma of whether we should stick to our position and risk falling far behind — or whether we should resume testing. Naturally, we were under increasing pressure from our military.

We finally decided to announce that if other countries refused to support the nuclear test ban, we would have no choice but to resume testing ourselves. We set a date for our next explosion. Literally a day or two before the resumption of our testing programme, I got a telephone call from Academician Sakharov. He addressed me in my capacity as the Chairman of the Council of Ministers, and he said he had a petition to present. The petition called on our government to cancel the scheduled nuclear explosion and not to engage in any further testing, at least not of the hydrogen bomb: 'As a scientist and as the designer of the hydrogen bomb, I know what harm these explosions can bring down on the head of mankind'.

Sakharov went on in that vein, pleading with me not to allow our military to conduct any further tests. He was obviously guided by moral and humanistic considerations. I knew him and was profoundly impressed by him. Everyone was. He was, as they say, a crystal of morality among our scientists. I'm sure he had none but the best of motives. He was devoted to the idea that science should bring peace and prosperity to the world, that it should help preserve and improve the conditions for human life. He hated the thought that science might be used to destroy life, to contaminate the atmosphere, to kill people slowly by radioactive poisoning. However, he went too far in thinking that he had the right to decide whether the bomb he had developed could ever be used in the future.

'Comrade Sakharov', I said, 'you must understand my position. My responsibilities in the post I hold do not allow me to cancel the tests. Our Party and government have already made abundantly clear that we would like nothing better than to suspend nuclear testing forever. Our leadership has already unilaterally discontinued nuclear testing and called on the United States and other countries to follow our example for the good of all mankind. But we got no answer. The Americans wouldn't listen to our proposals. As a scientist, surely you know that they've gone right on conducting their tests? If we don't test our own bombs, how will we know whether they work or not?'

He wasn't satisfied. He still insisted that we not resume our own testing.

I wanted to be absolutely frank with him: 'Comrade Sakharov, believe me, I deeply sympathise with your point of view. But as the man responsible for the security of our country, I have not right to do what you're asking me. For me to cancel the tests would be a crime against our state. I'm sure you know what kind of suffering was inflicted on our people during World War II? We can't risk the lives of our people again by giving our adversary a free hand to develop new means of destruction. Can't you understand that? To agree to what you are suggesting would spell doom for our country. Please understand that I simply cannot accept your plea; we must continue our tests.'

My arguments didn't change his mind, and his didn't change mine; but that was to be expected. Looking back on the affair, I feel Sakharov had the wrong attitude. Obviously he was of two minds. On the one hand, he had wanted to help his country defend itself against imperialist aggression. On the other hand, once he'd made it possible for us to develop the bomb, he was afraid of seeing it put to use. I think perhaps he was afraid of having his name associated with the possible implementation of the bomb. In other words, the scientist in him saw his patriotic duty and performed it well, while the pacifist in him made him hesitate. I have nothing against pacifists — or at least I *won't* have anything against them if and when we create conditions which make war impossible. But as long as we live in a world in which we have to keep both eyes open lest the imperialists gobble us up, then pacifism is a dangerous sentiment.

This conflict between Sakharov and me left a lasting imprint on us both. I took it as evidence that he didn't fully understand what was in the best interests of the state, and therefore from that moment on I was somewhat on my guard with him. I hope that the time will come when Comrade Sakharov will see the correctness of my position — if not now, then some time in the future.

We discussed Sakharov's petition in the leadership and decided to go ahead with the test. The bomb made an immensely powerful blast. The world had never seen such an explosion before. Our scientists calculated in advance that the force of the bomb would equal 50 million tons of TNT. That was the theory. In actual fact, the explosion turned out to be equivalent to 57 million tons. It was colossal, just incredible! Our experts later explained to me that if you took into account the shock wave and the radioactive contamination of the air, then the bomb produced as much destruction as 100 million tons of TNT.

I asked our scientists where we could use the bomb in case of war. I wanted to have a concrete idea about what destruction of this magnitude really meant. I was told that we wouldn't be able to bomb West Germany with a 57-megaton bomb because the prevailing westerly winds would blow the fallout over the German Democratic Republic, inflicting damage both on the civilian population and our own armed forces stationed there. However, we would not jeopardise ourselves or our allies if we dropped the bomb on England, Spain, France, or the United States.

It was a terrifying weapon. It gave us an opportunity to exert moral pressure on those who were conducting aggressive policies against the Soviet Union. We developed and tested the hydrogen bomb not in preparation for an attack, but for defence of our country against those who might attack us.''

Had we in the West known of these exchanges at the time they took place, would not the movement for nuclear disarmament have gained enormous strength from them? Indeed, Sakharov's memoirs record another protest, which would have given heart to everyone in the British Campaign for Nuclear Disarmament, if it had then been published:

"Another and no less dramatic episode occurred in 1962. The Ministry, acting basically from bureaucratic interests, issued instructions to proceed with a routine test explosion that was actually useless from the technical point of view. The explosion was to be powerful, so that the number of anticipated victims was colossal. Realising the unjustifiable, criminal nature of this plan, I made desperate efforts to stop it. This went on for several weeks — weeks that, for me, were full of tension. On the eve of the test I phoned the minister and threatened to resign. The minister replied: 'We're not holding you by the throat'. I was able to put a phone call through to Ashkabad, where Khrushchev was stopping on that particular day, and begged him to intervene. The next day I had a talk with one of Khrushchev's close advisers. But by then the time for the test had already been moved up to an earlier hour, and the carrier aircraft had already transported its burden to the designated point for the explosion. The feeling of impotence and fright that seized me on that day has remained in my memory ever since, and it has worked much change in me as I moved toward my present attitude."

Of course, Sakharov has sometimes changed his mind on these questions, which is hardly surprising, given their awe-inspiring finality. He records his role in the early limitation of nuclear testing:

"In 1962 I visited the minister of the atomic industry, who at that time was in a suburban government sanatorium together with the deputy minister of foreign affairs, and presented an important idea that had been brought to my attention by one of my friends. By then, talks on the banning of nuclear testing had already been going on for several years, the stumbling block being the difficulty of monitoring underground explosions. But radioactive contamination is caused only by explosions in the atmosphere, in space, and in the ocean. Therefore, limiting the agreement to banning tests in these three environments would solve both problems (contamination and monitoring). It should be noted that a similar proposal had previously been made by President Eisenhower, but at the time it had not accorded with the thinking of the Soviet side. In 1963 the so-called Moscow Treaty, in which this idea was realised, was concluded on the initiative of Khrushchev and Kennedy. It is possible that my initiative was of help in this historic act."

It is in this context that we should evaluate what he says in his letter to Academician Alexandrov. This letter seems to me to adopt a better position that that which was advanced by Sakharov earlier in his book *My Country and the World*, in what he explicitly calls for the support of the agreements reached at SALT II: in his essay on Problems of Disarmament, he opposed unilateral disarmament by the West, because this would "create a dangerous disturbance of the existing nuclear balance". But his concrete programme for disarmament in that essay is well worth detailed examination, even though many of us would like to question what is meant by the "existing nuclear balance". This formula appears in the letter to Alexandrov, when he writes that genuine disarmament is possible "only on an initial basis of strategic balance of power". The obvious question which arises is: how is this balance to be evaluated? Differences in weapons technology mean that the arms race inevitably takes the form of a game of leapfrog. Each new horrific weapon provokes an answering horror, but the response cannot simply be imitative. . . . In this dynamic situation there can be no such thing as a precise "balance". To choose to develop one weapon is to choose not to develop another, and since the different power centres make different choices, they will always be differentially armed in different departments.

In any case, Sakharov has not fully grasped the threat which arises from the developing doctrine of "limited war". He perceives a part of the problem when he speaks of the "Soviet destruction of strategic equilibrium in Europe". He does not apparently perceive the NATO destruction of that equilibrium, represented especially in the decision to deploy Pershing II missiles, which are a potent threat to the Soviet Union.

As you know, our reaction to the development of euro-strategic confrontation is to call for the creation of a nuclear weapons-free zone in the whole of Europe, East and West, between the territories of the super powers. We think that this will remove the incentive of the super powers to believe that they could fight a proxy war in our continent. It will also sober them in negotiations, because each will be aware that the others' missiles will be henceforth primarily targeted upon its own territory.

I don't know whether Academician Sakharov can receive accurate information on the issues we are discussing. You are perfectly aware already that the only English language newspaper which is on general sale in Moscow is the *Morning Star,* and that issues of this newspaper are commonly suppressed whenever it contains matter which the Soviet censorship regards as damaging. No doubt it is possible to receive foreign language broadcasts in Gorky: but you and I would not like to depend on these for our information about world events because they are commonly propagandistic and sometimes inaccurate. We don't know whether the Academician has received our recent letters or not, but we do know that earlier letters we sent him were not delivered, because we received compensation from the Post Office for their "loss".

Sakharov is obviously misinformed about the Soviet policy on oil supplies to the West: the CIA itself recently published a correction to earlier political estimates which it made on this matter; and none of us would be surprised if the Soviet Union were not to seek to offer further energy supplies to the West as a means of raising revenue and developing its economy. However, if Sakharov were able to discuss freely, many of these mistakes would be corrected quickly. They are the results of internal exile, not of personal prejudice.

In my opinion, you owe a second letter to Sakharov: but that should be addressed to the Soviet authorities, interceding on his behalf against the constraints to which he is objecting.

Yours sincerely,
Ken Coates.

CHAPTER SEVEN

Across the Berlin Wall

*On Good Friday 1982 I went to Berlin with Michael Meacher, MP.
The purpose of our visit, and its sad results, are described in what
follows. This account, which we jointly signed, was offered to* The
Guardian, *but not published there.*

We arrived in Berlin on Good Friday, and we were shivering when
we approached Checkpoint Charlie to cross into the East. The
formalities were perfunctory, and our teeth were not rattling in our
heads for fear, but because the temperature was 10 degrees below
that in London, and we were not dressed for the weather.

We had come to see Robert Havemann, the distinguished East
German scientist, who had become the main independent voice of
the peace movement in his half of divided Germany. We knew that
he was gravely ill, but we were not to know that he was to die that
evening, at 9 o'clock, before we could keep our appointment with
him.

Havemann has been described in the West as a "dissident", but
this is a travesty of his much more complex position. He was a
democrat and a passionate socialist. So he regarded the
expropriation of private capitalism in German industry as a major
achievement of the East German Government, and thought that
this marked the East German Democratic Republic as the most
advanced state ever to exist in Germany. But he fought its extensive
bureaucracy with all his powers, and was a tireless critic of each
and all the repressive acts of "his" Government. The result was
that he spent much of his last decade under house arrest, launching
appeals for peace to World and European statesmen, and using his
scientific knowledge to understand and explain the dangers which
are inherent in the newest round of the arms race.

The Russell Foundation had published much of Havemann's
most recent writing, and we were looking forward very much to

Ken Coates and Michael Meacher in Berlin.

meeting him. Beyond doubt, had his conscience permitted it, he could have been made entirely welcome in the West. But like Socrates, he chose to live with and suffer the implications of his own ideas. His loss will affect all Europe, as well as both Germanies.

Under the shadow of his death, we spent all the evening hours of Good Friday with Pastor Rainer Eppelmann, a loyal friend of Havemann's, and an initiator of the Berlin Appeal for Nuclear Disarmament (printed below). This courageous document has been canvassed not only in churches, but in factories, colleges, hospitals and schools, and is part of the upsurge of pacifist feeling throughout both Germanies. In the East, the church plays a particular role, and has anchored its message to the text from Micah in the Old Testament: "And they shall beat the swords into ploughshares".

Eppelmann is a slight, balding, intense man. His commitment and his courage are inextricably bound up with his modesty. He received us at his house, where we were furnished by his wife with a constant supply of strong tea for a very long and concentrated discussion. Their children were playing in the next room, and, at first sight, our interview did not seem to be overshadowed by the pressure of a jealous state.

But only two or three days before our arrival, Eppelmann had been summoned to a meeting at the security offices, where he was warned that if he persisted in his unlicensed activities he would have to face the consequences (which could be up to a 10-year sentence for publicly challenging the State's "peace politics"). His previous encounters with these authorities have been widely reported in the West. Of course, the Berlin Appeal does call for the withdrawal of all occupation troops from Germany, and for non-intervention by the victors of World War II in the internal affairs of the two German states. Unintimidated, Eppelmann insists upon his right to discuss this question with Christians, pacifists and disarmers in the West, and hopes that prominent spokesmen of the peace movement will go to East Germany in order to meet their independent-minded opposite numbers in Magdeburg, Dresden and Berlin.

Two weeks before our visit, the Protestant churches said that they stood behind the alternative peace movement, and that they supported the campaign symbol 'Swords into Ploughshares'. This stand, Eppelmann informed us, was to be publicly announced in a letter to be read out in all the churches in Berlin Brandenburg on Easter Sunday. Several factories have also shown their support for the churches' view of the Berlin Appeal. So far, the Appeal has been signed very widely, but it has not yet received the support of prominent people. Of course, some people may fear the loss of privileges, such as the right of foreign travel, if they endorse so "subversive" a message.

The peace movement, Eppelmann told us, represents one of the cases "where one has to achieve a better balance between acting for Jesus and making an adjustment to the state". Even now a majority of church leaders are backing him, which was unexpected as little as six months ago. People in his own church, who strongly opposed him as little as eight weeks ago, are now more friendly, because "they were not stupid — they can see how the atmosphere is changing".

The churches are dependent on the benevolence of the State in order to continue as now, but in a conflict Eppelmann believes the State will find much more room for compromise. Of course there is a danger for the state that if the Peace agitation gets a strong hold, and if the implications of its Appeal were actually to lead to the denuclearisation of Germany and the withdrawal of Pact forces, the position of the East German Government could be undermined (Solidarnosc in Poland is a great worry to the German Democratic Republic's officials). But events will be watched even more closely here (than in Poland), because there is another Germany.

On the other hand, Cruise and Pershing II are a real threat to the Soviets, and the GDR is torn between Soviet interests (in encouraging the Western peace movement as the best means to get the West not to deploy Cruise and Pershing) and its own interests in nipping the domestic peace movement in the bud. For the Berlin Appeal involves people whose interest is not only peace, but civil liberties too.

More than 2,000 signatures to the Berlin Appeal have already been collected, and the first 72 people to sign were all called in for interview by the authorities.

This raises a powerful point of principle for the Western peace movements, who must surely insist upon the right to free access to their Eastern opposite numbers, and upon freedom of travel across frontiers for all those engaged in supporting the work of disarmament.

Eppelmann himself strongly insisted that the growing support for the Berlin Appeal, the widely reported activities in Dresden, the upsurge of pacifist activity in Magdeburg and many similar unreported events did not constitute any organised "movement", but represented a spontaneous reaction to the worsening international situation. Of course, the churches are deeply concerned to apply Christian principles in a disordered world, but they are not offering any narrowly political challenge to the authorities.

Eppelmann would like to attend the European Nuclear Disarmament Convention in Brussels in July, which will assemble very many representatives from the different peace movements of Europe. But he is apprehensive that, if he did attend, some of his countrymen might like to see him kept out, forbidden to return home. Of course, the German Democratic Republic cultivates its reputation for welcoming "peace-fighters", so they would certainly lose something if they kept him out. Meantime, Eppelmann has asked the Church authorities in East Germany to initiate discussions with other Church leaders in neighbouring socialist countries, about the Berlin Appeal, and talks are soon to begin with Polish Protestant Church leaders.

Rainer Eppelmann is, at this moment, much less well-known in Western Europe than his friend, Robert Havemann. But, meeting as we did, in the last moments of Havemann's life, we became quite sure that Havemann's work will be continued and that Eppelmann will soon become a household name wherever the Western peace movement is gathering strength. As we crossed again through the slightly surreal world of the Checkpoint, we wondered whether this peace movement might soon be able to bring an end to the last war, at the same time that it helps prevent the next one.

Berlin Appeal: Peace Without Weapons

1

There is only one kind of war which could take place in Europe, nuclear war. The weapons stockpiled in the East and the West won't save us, but destroy us. We will all be long dead when the soldiers in their tanks and at the missile bases as well as the generals and politicians in their bunkers, on whose protection we have relied, are still living and continuing to destroy whatever remains.

2

If, therefore, we want to remain alive — away with all weapons! First of all: away with nuclear weapons! The whole of Europe must become a nuclear-free zone. We propose there should be negotiations between the governments of the two German states about the withdrawal of all nuclear weapons from German soil.

3

Divided Germany has become the deployment area for the two nuclear superpowers. We propose an end to this potentially fatal confrontation. The victors of World War II should finally negotiate peace treaties with both German states as was agreed in the Potsdam Treaty of 1945. Thereafter, the former allies should withdraw their occupational troops from Germany and agree on a policy of non-intervention in the internal affairs of the two German states.

4

We propose that the question of peace be discussed in an atmosphere of tolerance and recognition of the right of free expression. Every spontaneous public expression of the desire for peace should be supported and encouraged. We appeal to the public and our government to consider the following questions:

a. Should we not renounce the production, sale, and import of so-called war toys and games?

b. Should we not introduce lessons about peace problems in our schools instead of military instruction?

c. Should we not allow a social peace service for conscientious objectors instead of the present kind of alternative to military service?

d. Should we not relinquish all demonstrations of military strength in public and, instead, use our national celebrations for declaring the people's desire for peace?

e. Should we not do without our so-called civil defence exercises? Since there won't be any possibility of a meaningful civil defence in a nuclear war, the very real threat of nuclear warfare is made to seem less imminent by these exercises. Isn't it rather a method of psychological preparation for war?

Peace without weapons — that does not only mean ensuring our own survival. It also means finishing with the senseless waste of labour and national wealth on the production of arms and equipment for gigantic armies of young men who are thereby kept off productive work. Should we not help the starving all over the world instead of continuing to prepare for our own death?

Blessed are the meek: for they shall inherit the earth. (Jesus of Nazareth in his Sermon on the Mount).

The balance of fear has prevented nuclear war up to now only by postponing it till tomorrow. The nations of the world regard the approach of this tomorrow with dread. They are looking for new ways to secure the foundations of peace. The 'Berlin Appeal' is an expression of this wish. Think about it, make proposals to our politicians and everywhere discuss the question:

What will bring about peace; what will lead to war?

Please indicate your support by signing below.

Berlin,
25th January 1982

CHAPTER EIGHT

An Exchange of Open Letters with the Soviet Peace Committee

After the Brussels Convention for European Nuclear Disarmament, Mr Yuri Zhukov, of the Soviet Peace Committee, sent an open letter to European Peace Movements. I replied on behalf of the Russell Foundation. Both letters are reproduced in full.

The Soviet Peace Committee Criticises

36, Mira pr.
Moscow, USSR
December 1982

Dear Friends,
In our time as never before there is a need for a dialogue and mutual understanding among different peace forces.

We would like to share with you quite frankly some considerations about the prospects of the further development of the anti-war movement. We are prompted to do so by the disturbing development of the international situation.

The doctrine of a "crusade" against the Soviet Union and the other socialist countries taken up as the official creed by the present US administration leads, in practical terms, not only to a direct confrontation in the political, ideological and economic spheres. The leaders of the USA and NATO openly proclaim plans of nuclear warfare.

In Europe, in spite of the arms limitation talks currently held, preparations are under way for deploying a new generation of US nuclear missiles. Evidence has come up to the effect that three to four times as many Pershing II and cruise missiles as were envisaged by NATO's "double decision" of 1979 are being prepared for stationing. Moreover, the USA is intent on deploying Pershing II missiles, cruise missiles with nuclear warheads, and neutron weapons on the territory of Israel.

We believe the year 1983 when the deployment of US missiles in Western Europe is planned to begin to be especially important and in a sense crucial to the struggle for preventing this threat to peace and European security. And this is not just our view. More and more people in the West and in the East are becoming aware of the obvious truth that the dangerous international developments can only be stopped by joint and resolute mass actions of all those who are committed to peace. The anti-war movement everywhere is growing in strength and width and becoming an important factor of international politics, one that has to be heeded by all political parties and governments.

Yet, it is impossible to ignore the fact that there is a sharp increase in the actions by the opponents of peace forces, trying hard to neutralise the anti-war movement, disorientate the people in the movement and push them off the right way.

So far the peace champions of the various streams, movements and organisations both in the West and East have been coming out together for peace and disarmament, laying aside their ideological differences, however serious they might be. It is easy to see how much weaker their combined efforts would be if the anti-war movements were to set those differences as lines of demarcation between themselves, breeding enmity.

In this context one cannot but feel concerned about the discussions imposed by some persons and groups in order to eventually split the anti-war movement which is global by its nature and to infiltrate the "cold war" elements into it. The promoters of those discussions increasingly strive to turn anti-war forums into an arena of open ideological struggle by replacing the discussion of the major task of preventing nuclear war, a task that united all, with debates on issues that have nothing to do with this task.

In this connection we would like to share with you our impressions of the Convention for European Nuclear Disarmament that was held in Brussels last July on the initiative of the Bertrand Russell Foundation and the so-called Movement for European Nuclear Disarmament (END). Its organisers claim that the purpose of this event was to "rally the broad forces and groups within the mass anti-war movement on the basis of a wide discussion providing the groundwork for fruitful co-operation". This concept of co-operation among the peace forces in Europe can only be welcomed. However, the deliberations and the outcome of the Brussels Convention have shown that the true objective of its sponsors was not to rally but to disunite the anti-war movements.

Prior to the Convention a lengthy discussion took place among its sponsors as to whether they should invite representatives of the public organisations of the socialist countries. Finally the participation issue was resolved so that the right to take part in the conference was granted not to the real mass peace movements of the socialist countries but to a group of people who have left their countries and have nothing in common with the struggle for peace and who, while representing nobody, are busy disseminating hostile slanderous fabrications about the foreign and home policies of their former motherland. Only as an exception were some representatives of Yugoslavia, Romania and Hungary allowed to attend.

As a result the Convention was a West European rather than a European operation for all its sponsors' insistence on the latter. This was the start of overt actions aimed at disuniting the anti-war movement in Europe.

These actions have caused perplexity and protests among many participants in the Convention. Indeed, one can hardly seriously believe that the struggle for peace and security in Europe can be successfully pursued without the participation of millions of people living in Europe's socialist countries. Whatever may be claimed by the organisers of the Convention on this score, they actually make an attempt to isolate the West European anti-war movements and organisations from the real mass movements of peace champions in the socialist countries and to substitute them by certain individuals passed off as allies who are active not in the struggle for detente and disarmament but in undermining the socialist system.

The Convention is known to have been held under the slogan of achieving European nuclear disarmament. It is also known that the only nuclear power which has made an official statement that it stands for elimination of all nuclear weapons from the whole European continent is the Soviet Union. Naturally the Soviet public organisations as well as all candid peace champions abroad welcome and support this stand. And yet there are people who try to practise discrimination against these organisations describing them as "official" and "dependent" on the grounds that they support the peace policy of their government.

We, as many other people, now query what are these people actually striving for — the elimination of nuclear weapons or rather the elimination of a united universal anti-war movement, the participation in which is determined both in the West and East not by anti or "pro-government" stands but by its anti-militarist, anti-war positions.

It is a truly monstrous design to try and use the banner of peace in order to draw the anti-war movement into what is to all intents and purposes a "cold war" against the public in socialist countries and to lead them along this path to the impasse of anti-Sovietism and anti-communism. These actions cannot be justified by the assertions of the Convention organisers that they wish to be "neutral" to both "superpowers" and strive to be equally removed from their foreign policies.

At present active preparations are known to be under way for the second Convention to be held in West Berlin in May 1983. We have hoped that its organisers would have analysed all negative aspects of the Brussels meeting and come up with a different, more democratic, politically balanced and responsible approach. In that case the Soviet public organisations which abide by the principle that co-operation must be sought among all peace forces with no exception, would have been ready to take part in the preparatory work and the deliberations of the Convention. That is why we agreed to hold consultative meetings with representatives of the West Berlin "Working Group for a Nuclear-free Europe" who are in charge of the practical preparations for the second Convention.

We sincerely hoped that we would find, as a result of these meetings, a mutually acceptable basis for co-operation leading to a truly constructive dialogue between the peace forces representing not only the West but also the East at the Convention itself. However, contacts with the Convention organisers confirmed our worst apprehensions as to its character and orientation.

Our talks in Moscow in October 1982 with the representatives of the West Berlin "Working Group for a Nuclear-free Europe" — J. Graalfs, W. Grunwald, G. Gumlich. T. Schweisfurth and R. Steinke — and the documents available to us made us quite certain that things boil down to a deliberate attempt to distract the attention of the peace-loving public away from the main source of deadly peril to the European nations, viz. plans to deploy a new generation of nuclear missiles in Western Europe in 1983. It has become obvious that the issue of a nuclear-free Europe is largely a rubber-stamp measure put on the agenda as a concession to the demands of really mass anti-war organisations working against the deployment of new US missiles.

The assertion of the organisers of the West Berlin Convention that they are intent on forming an "anti-bloc" movement for "equal responsibility of both blocs and above all, the USA and USSR" does not hold water. They wilfully elude any concrete analysis of the policies of certain states and hush up a well-known fact that the Warsaw Treaty Organisation has repeatedly made an official proposal to simultaneously dissolve both blocs and as for NATO leaders, they are reluctant even to discuss the matter.

The leaders of the Bertrand Russell Peace Foundation and the Movement for European Nuclear Disarmament somehow keep silent about the following significant fact. In a well-known Appeal for European Nuclear Disarmament of 28 April 1980, which is put forward as a political platform of the Convention, the authors have stated that both sides, i.e. the East and West, bear the equal blame and along with this they have appealed to the USA and USSR to remove all nuclear weapons from the European soil and specifically demanded that the USSR stop the production of Soviet medium-range SS20 missiles and the USA abandon its decision to deploy Pershing II and cruise missiles in Western Europe. They also appealed to both powers to ratify SALT II.

Since the publication of the Appeal the positions of the USSR and USA towards these demands have become definite. The USSR, as it has been mentioned, has come forward with a proposal of a real "zero option" — to eliminate both medium-range weapons and tactical nuclear weapons from the European territory. It has stopped the stationing of medium-range missiles capable of hitting targets in Europe and even started a unilateral reduction of their quantity. The USSR has always been for the ratification and implementation of SALT II. Finally, the USSR has come out with a historic initiative pledging a unilateral obligation of non-use of nuclear weapons first.

However, the USA has taken an entirely opposite stand on all these issues, rejecting all the demands of the peace forces.

The leaders of the Bertrand Russell Foundation and the Movement for European Nuclear Disarmament make it appear that they are unware of these facts and keep foisting on others their concept of "equal responsibility". We are firmly convinced that this concept is aimed at the disorientation, demobilisation and undermining of the anti-war movement and is called upon to conceal and justify an aggressive militarist policy of the USA and NATO.

It has become known that the organisers plan to bring a so-called "German question" into discussions at the Convention, thus trying to challenge the inviolability of the post-war European frontiers and to violate the letter and spirit of the Helsinki Final Act.

The only way we can regard such political manoeuvres is as an attempt to revise the well-known agreements between the Federal Republic of Germany and its neighbours and the status of West Berlin.

It is not at all coincidental that the "Working Group" is planning to hold an international symposium in West Berlin next June on the occasion of the 30th anniversary of the abortive counter-revolutionary coup staged in the GDR in 1953. What is it but an interference in the internal affairs of the GDR, and in effect a provocative attempt to force onto the anti-war movement an issue which has nothing to do with the movement for a nuclear-free Europe and resuscitates the revanchist sentiments.

We cannot agree with the anti-democratic stand taken by the organisers of the West Berlin Convention on the issue of preparation for this forum. We were told that the participation in the preparatory committee had been restricted only to those who adhere to the above Appeal incorporating a number of provisions unacceptable to many anti-war organisations, including ourselves. Moreover, as it has been shown above, some of the provisions of the Appeal are simply outdated. While clinging to this condition, the organisers of the Convention obviously try to use it for a selective approach in choosing the would-be participants among the individuals and organisations.

Answering the question of the possibility for the Peace Committees of the socialist countries to participate in the Convention, the representatives of the West Berlin "Working Group" have evasively declared that it is practically impossible to solve this question within the framework of the Liaison Committee. How are they going to organise an East-West dialogue at the Convention? It turned out that they intended to selectively send out personal invitations to individual public figures in the socialist countries to attend in "personal capacity" even then confining them to an observer status. This makes us certain that the Convention organisers simply fear the appearance of real opponents and therefore prefer to engage in anti-socialist propaganda in the absence of plenipotentiaries of public opinion in the Soviet Union and other socialist countries.

Neither can we agree with the fact that virtually all major decisions with regard to the preparations and proceedings at the Convention are taken by a limited group of people (K. Coates, L. Castellina, J. Lambert and J. Graalfs), while others are assigned the role of mute partners.

We are convinced that the orientation which the organisers try to lend to the Convention and the methods of its preparation preclude the possibility of a fruitful All-European dialogue, which would be conducive to expanding co-operation of peace forces, who hunger for it in the present menacing international situation. On the contrary, all this will contribute to fomenting a "cold war" among the participants in the anti-war movement in Europe threatening to push this movement backwards. Naturally we shall not be a party to this wrecking undertaking.

We thought it necessary to let you know our stand with complete frankness so as to avoid misunderstanding or idle speculation. Our meetings and talks show that many public figures and organisations both in Eastern and Western Europe share our opinion or hold similar views with regard to the Convention.

For our part, we are going to continue working towards a better mutual understanding and joint actions of the public movements in the East and in the West for our common goal, that of averting the danger of nuclear war and freeing our continent of all nuclear weapons.

Your sincerely,
Yuri Zhukov,
President, Soviet Peace Committee.

The Russell Foundation Replies

1st February, 1983

Dear Mr Zhukov,
We have just received your letter to Western Peace Movements, dated 2 December 1982. You did not send it to this Foundation, against which you raise serious complaints. We regret that you have not discussed these with us, since there are several points in which your letter errs, and which could have been clarified had you approached us. Now we are in the position of replying to an open letter, so we feel sure you will forgive us if we reply with a frankness equal to your own.

First, we must say that it is a pity that your letter so plainly contradicts the spirit of the important new initiatives taken by Mr

Andropov and your Government during the past few weeks. During this time we have noted the very significant speech of 21 December, with its new offer concerning the further reduction of Soviet SS20 missiles against that of British and French equivalent weaponry. We find this entirely reasonable, and unequivocally support it. We also welcome the proposed "no-first-use" agreement on conventional weapons, which we see as a worthwhile confidence-building measure. We further very much support the UN decision on a nuclear freeze, carried with your Government's adherence.

We also welcome new initiatives to normalise Soviet-Chinese relations. Not all, by any means, of these proposals are totally new in themselves, but as a package they give us real hope that a new policy in the USSR will re-open new and serious impulses to disarmament. In none of these matters are we your Government's critics. In fact, we think Mr Andropov has properly seized the initiative, and all pressure should be brought upon the United States and our own Government to reciprocate.

Yet, for all our hopes in this field, we still think that non-alignment is the proper course for our peace movements, and ultimately for all the European countries. This is not, as you wrongly assume, because we hold the two superpowers to be "equally" responsible for the present state of the arms race. In fact we disagree with this view, and have frequently said so. Our main criticism has always been addressed to our own Government, against which we assert all our constitutional rights of opposition, because this is the main authority whose behaviour we may hope to influence. Nonetheless it is our opinion that blame of different kinds does historically attach to each bloc, and we do not wish simply to exchange blocs, but to make possible a genuine, and reciprocal, exit from the entire system of bloc divisions in our continent. In no way does this aspiration threaten the reasonable interests of the USSR, or the legitimate concerns of the USA. We seek amity with both powers in a changed world in which co-operation replaces conflict and the threat of the employment of force.

1983 is a crossroads for Europe and the world, as we have said consistently. The installation of the Pershing II and cruise missiles by NATO we see as a real threat to your country, which will within the logic of the arms race bring down further threats on our heads. Escalation of this already insane arms race imperils all mankind. That is the basis of our Appeal, although you never mention it.

What is your alternative? Our Appeal concerns the peoples of that Europe which is sandwiched between yourselves and the Americans. It must attract their majority support if it is to succeed. If your offer them peace instead on the sole basis of unswerving support for your own Government's policies in every field of world affairs, how many will agree? Obviously, this will depend in part on what those policies are. In the late 1950s and early '60s, your Government won many friends, who had originally been highly suspicious of the previous regime. One of these was our founder, Bertrand Russell, who recorded the progress of his thinking in his Autobiography:

> "In the late '40s and early '50s, I had been profoundly impressed by the horror of Stalin's dictatorship, which had led me to believe that there would be no easy resolution of the cold war. I later came to see that for all his ruthlessness, Stalin had been very conservative. I had assumed, like most people in the West, that his tyranny was expansionist, but later evidence made it clear that it was the West that had given him Eastern Europe as part of the spoils of the Second World War, and that, for the most part, he had kept his agreements with the West. After his death, I earnestly hoped that the world would come to see the folly and danger of living permanently in the shadow of nuclear weapons. If the contenders for world supremacy could be kept apart, perhaps the neutral nations could introduce the voice of reason into international affairs. It was a small hope, for I overestimated the power of the neutrals. Only rarely, as with Nehru in Korea, did they manage to add significant weight to pressures against the cold war.
>
> The neutrals continued to embody my outlook, in that I consider human survival more important than ideology. But a new danger came to the fore. It became obvious that Russia no longer entertained hope of world-empire, but that this hope had now passed over to the United States. As my researches into the origins and circumstances of the war in Vietnam showed, the United States was embarking upon military adventures which increasingly replaced war with Russia as the chief threat to the world. The fanaticism of America's anti-communism, combined with its constant search for markets and raw materials, made it impossible for any serious neutral to regard America and Russia as equally dangerous to the world."

Russell's view of Soviet policy was subsequently partially changed again, mainly by the invasion of Czechoslovakia, which did much to distance you from many over here who want peace, and also from socialists and communists in many countries. Foreign reactions to the Soviet Union are only partly conditioned by bellicose propaganda, which is undoubtedly powerful, and from the attentions of which we suffer also. They are also formed by what your Government positively does. Now the Soviet Union is one of the major powers, not a beseiged island attempting to pioneer new social forms. Paradoxically this means you can no longer rely on the uncritical support which was widely aroused in the earlier, embattled and heroic days of the foundation of your State. Today a peace movement composed of only your uncritical admirers in the West would consist of relatively few people, who would in no way constitute a force adequate to prevent the installation of cruise and Pershing II missiles, or to compel the United States and others to negotiate seriously to reverse the arms race. To fulfill these tasks, only a non-aligned movement has any hope of generating support on a wide enough scale. And the price of a non-aligned movement is that it is not aligned. The more constructively your Government is able to behave, the more such a movement will support you. The stronger it becomes, the more scope you will have for such constructive behaviour.

Thus, unless you were perversely to wish, for doctrinal reasons or whyever, to be able to act as arbitrarily and unkindly as possible, you ought to hope against hope that the non-aligned movement will grow. It is genuinely in both our interests. Not only may it help bring disarmament nearer, but it may also create more favourable conditions within which you may concentrate on your own peaceful renewal, and on carrying through safely and in optimal conditions whatever reforms you may think desirable and progressive. A non-aligned movement all over Europe, with millions of supporters, would mean that we, too, recovered a freedom of action which has been denied to us whilst our predominant modes of thought have been locked into the blocs. In what imaginable way does this threaten you? How does it "provoke" you? As you rightly say, the Soviet Union has many times affirmed such a European perspective as its own. Why, when we assert it, and seek to give it material embodiment, does it suddenly "divide the peace movement" and serve the interests of NATO?

Some people over here accuse us of precisely the opposite intentions. In our peace movements, as you know, there exist many different minorities, and much dissent, about some of which you are well informed. We will happily assist you to gain even fuller information, if you would like it. This dissent is our strength. It enables pacifists, socialists, church people, communists, greens and all kinds of special groups to work together, not simply, as you put it, "laying aside" their differences, but actually celebrating those differences in common cause. Such differences will be plainly apparent, in profusion, at the Berlin Convention next May. That is why we invited you to come, to share in the experience, and to discuss with us. All of us will learn from it.

But why, then, could we not ask you to co-organise the event? Because it is organised by signatories of the April 1980 Appeal which your letter misunderstands and indeed denounces. The agenda is our agenda, an agenda of non-alignment. Whilst we have already informed you that we would welcome you among us, you must surely appreciate that we cannot surrender our own joint control over what is our platform. Do you always expect people to agree to such conditions when you visit them? If so, your travels must be rather restricted. The fraternal delegates of the CPSU do not tell the British Labour Party Conference that they must be invited to serve on the Conference Arrangements Committee before they will come, and Soviet Trade Unions are quite willing to visit other trade union bodies without making any demands whatever upon them. Why do you believe that the Peace Movement should be an exception to this rule? Surely there is no doubt about what you would say if we requested reciprocal rights concerning the agenda of your own meetings? No, this is not a serious proposal. We are what we are, and you are what you are, and we are willing to talk if you find it useful. But if we offer you friendship, it would be friendship without subservience.

Now let me deal with detailed matters on which you are wrongly informed. Your report our discussion about Eastern European participation at Brussels, saying that we invited "a group of people who have left their countries and have nothing in common with the struggle for peace and who, while representing nobody, are busy disseminating hostile slanderous fabrications about the foreign and home policies of their former motherland". Which people are these? We do not know them. We in fact invited all signatories to our Appeal. One of these is Zhores Medvedev, who was the only Russian to speak in a panel discussion. So far was he from "disseminating hostile slanderous fabrications" about the USSR, that many of the European communists who were present thought he was unduly supportive of official Soviet positions. This was not our view, since we shared most of his reasoning. It is difficult to see how you could have arrived at the view expressed in your letter, had you been aware of what Dr Medvedev actually said.

"Only as an exception", you say, were some representatives of Yugoslavia "allowed to attend". This is far from the truth. The Yugoslav League for Peace, Independence and Equality of Peoples was among the earlier signatories to our Appeal, and they participated, and will participate, as of right in all our deliberations. They honoured us by sending their immediate past President, Bogdan Osolnik, together with another member of their presidency. As the premier non-aligned peace movement in Europe, they have our deep respect. Also present were distinguished Romanian and Hungarian participants, both of whom played an active and very constructive role in the workshops they chose to attend. Ask them. If their experiences are evidence of "overt actions aimed at disuniting the anti-war movement" then it would be difficult to see how to strive for peace on any basis other than one which would reduce all the European movements to miniscule proportions. Since neither we nor you want that, we had better think again.

You make much of the alleged preoccupation of our forthcoming Convention with the "German Question". In fact there is no such preoccupation. The Liaison Committee has allocated one seminar amongst two dozen or so to the consideration of the issue of German Disarmament, which is raised by some German peace activists, not as a slogan of revanchism, but as a call for the denuclearisation of both Germanies. Is this such a bad idea? If so, will the fact not become apparent in a free and open discussion? How do you imagine a mass peace movement can reach consensus about its goals without such exchanges? Concerning the meeting of 17 June of which you speak, we know nothing. Our Convention is scheduled from 9 May to 15 May. We are not involved in any subsequent gathering. If you had asked us, you would instantly have discovered this fact.

Then you go on to criticise the organisation of the Liaison Committee which organises the Convention. Here your remarks are equally ill-informed. This Committee involves nearly a hundred people from more than a score of countries. It controls the Conventions in every detail. The four joint secretaries who you name do not meet separately, have no special powers, and are charged solely with the convening of meetings. Why does all this alarm you? It is a completely transparent process, both in its unity and its diversity. If you allow yourself to feel threatened by it, you are suffering from empty phobias.

We do not wish here to exchange detailed opinions about which particular aspects of Soviet policy merit support, and which opposition. One day, we hope, we will talk about it. But we should also talk about your misperception of our own attitudes to the many wrongs done in the "Western" part of the world. Surely you cannot have been at your desk at *Pravda* for as long as you have been without being aware of some aspects or other of our own consistent opposition to all forms of imperialism, of our efforts to assist colonial struggles for independence, or of our general defence of civil freedoms and political prisoners in countries East, West and Neutral.

Your letter does your Committee a disservice by offering such unsubtle attempts to represent us as agents provocateurs in the service of the Western powers. We have no doubt that you will quickly be disabused of these opinions when you begin to receive replies from those to whom you have addressed your remarks. They will provoke dismay among many of your well-wishers.

Now we begin a new year. Let us propose that instead of writing *about* each other, we write *to* each other, and see what emerges.

Yours sincerely,
Ken Coates.

CHAPTER NINE

The Peace Movement
and Socialism*

I. Introductory

In 1980, facing up to a renewed upsurge of militarism, a number of us joined forces to launch an appeal for European Nuclear Disarmament. This began with a warning. "We are entering the most dangerous decade in history", it said. There is a good deal of new evidence to show that this appreciation was exact, containing not a milligram of exaggeration.

But there is now also confirmation that problems call forth responses, and indeed that people are nowadays more ingenious and inventive than they used to be. The European Peace Movement, which has become a plain fact, has not only assembled its millions of adherents, but it has also unlocked the most remarkable talents and set loose a vast nuclear fusion of human energies.

In the early days, *New Left Review* gave impetus to this process, when it published Edward Thompson's challenging paper on exterminism, which subsequently provoked an important discussion in several major countries at once.

Now again, NLR has sought to bring this argument to a new level, by opening the question of the relation between socialism and nuclear war, and the interaction of socialist and peace movements. Ernest Mandel (Number 140, September/October 1983) is addressing a crucial theme, and that is why I think it right to take issue with him on a whole series of contingent matters. Of course it is easy to identify some areas of agreement, which it is also proper to mark out. This paper is not intended as a polemic response: I have a deep respect for Ernest Mandel, who has enriched my world for nearly 30 years of argumentative friendship. Rather, I seek to worry at some of the issues which, both of us agree, matter, and to share my worries. So impenetrable is the territory of present travails that I doubt whether any individual can map it entire, leave

*This article was reprinted by *New Left Review* as a response to Ernest Mandel's: 'Socialism and Nuclear War'.

◀ *Ernest Mandel.*

alone point the way across it. That is why we must talk to one another, and also learn to listen.

In what follows I seek to discuss Mandel's view of imperialism, his assessment of the interactions between labour movements and war in general, and his assessment of the threat of nuclear war and the use of nuclear weapons. This requires some consideration of the argument about the sociology of superpowers, and the notion of exterminism. In turn, this task involves us in looking at the degree of social control over nuclear choices in the military field, the extent of accountability within national nuclear forces, and the linkages within alliances. Only within such a framework, I think, can we appreciate the tasks of the socialist movement and the peace campaign in their true convergence, which I believe needs careful exploration and development.

II: Socialism or Barbarism?

That the earliest socialists were originally themselves a peace movement ought not to be in dispute. We have already recalled the prescient warning of Marx and Engels in 1848:

> "The history of all hitherto existing society is the history of class struggles.
>
> Freeman and slave, patrician and plebian, lord and serf, guildmaster and journeyman, in a word, oppressor and oppressed, stood in constant opposition to one another, carried on an uninterrupted, now hidden, now open fight, a fight that each time ended, either in a revolutionary reconstitution of society at large, or in the common ruin of the contending classes."[1]

One hundred years after the death of Karl Marx, these opening words of *The Communist Manifesto* sound to many people more like a premonition of doom than the hopeful exhortation they were intended to be. "The common ruin of the contending classes" no longer presents itself as a distant prospect, but must appear as a distinct probability as we peer at one another between the nuclear emplacements which sprout all over Europe in the middle of the 1980s.

In the early months of the First World War, writing in the prison to which she was confined for defending Marx's internationalism, Rosa Luxemburg composed her pamphlet *The Crisis in German Social Democracy,* which subsequently became better known as *The Junius Pamphlet.*[2] In this tract, she harked back to Engels' statement "Capitalist society faces a dilemma, either an advance to socialism or a reversion to barbarism''. For Luxemburg, "This world war means a reversion to barbarism . . . either the triumph of imperialism and the destruction of all culture . . . depopulation, desolation, degeneration, a vast cemetery; or the victory of socialism''. Those who drew the human balance sheet of that first World War could not fail to confirm Luxemburg's appreciation of it. While her pamphlet was being clandestinely printed, the battle of Verdun was raging over a 20-mile front. A five-mile movement along this front cost 281,000 German lives and 315,000 French lives. On 10 July 1916, Luxemburg was re-arrested, so that she was again in prison during the battle of the Somme, which was continued until 14 November, costing 419,604 British and 194,451 French casualties. German losses were estimated at half a million.[3]

Over four dreadful years, the unimaginable carnage cost an estimated 272,970 million dollars. "Barbarism" is in common parlance a mild description for such universal mayhem: although it is grossly unfair to real barbarians, for whom slaughter was a heavy physical labour, unameliorated by the mechanical arts. Today, the process of slaughter is more efficient than ever. Vastly increased military expenditures bring within reach casualty lists besides which the First World War seems almost a benevolent event. Luxemburg did not believe that the barbarism she denounced would amount to "the common ruin of the contending classes": "we are not lost", she said, "and we will be victorious if we have not forgotten how to learn''. In 1918 there were still generations left with time to learn.[4]

But only 20 years later most of these lessons had been forgotten. During the six years from September 1939, 70 million men were enrolled in the combatant armed forces, and seventeen million of these were killed. A sure mark of the advance of the barbarians is that "more civilians were killed than soldiers - some by aerial bombardment, others murdered by the Germans as partisans or hostages, many more murdered gratuitously in execution of Nazi racial doctrine, many perishing from hardship and starvation, while carrying out forced labour in Germany or when beseiged at Leningrad and elsewhere.''[5]

A.J.P. Taylor offers us statistics of the national losses: 5.8 million Polish men, women and children were murdered by the Germans, alongside 300,000 Polish soldiers killed. Poland thus suffered a population loss of 15 per cent. Six million Soviet soldiers were killed in battle, and 14 million civilians and soldiers were murdered during the German occupation. The USSR thus lost 10 per cent of its population. One-third of the one-and-a-half million Yugoslavs who were killed were combatants: the rest, civilians. Four-and-a-half million Germans were killed in battle, and nearly 600,000 civilians died under air bombardment. A million Japanese died in battle, and 600,000 civilians under the bombs. Figures for the slaughter in China are harder to establish: between three and thirteen million people, Taylor guesses, "more from general hardship than in actual fighting". A dreadful famine carried off millions in India. 200,000 French soldiers were killed, with twice as many non-soldiers. 300,000 Italians died in combat, "half of them fighting as regular soldiers on the German side, half fighting as partisans on the side of the allies". As many British soldiers perished, together with 62,000 civilians who died in the Blitzkrieg. The United States "came off lightest: 300,000 military dead, divided almost equally between the European and Asiatic theatres of operation, and no civilians".

The steady progress of what are now called "conventional" weapons was already, by 1945, filling hecatombs with the civilian dead. The bombers who visited Tokyo on 8 March 1945 destroyed 83,000 people, or 21,000 more than the total of those who perished under the bombs which fell on Britain during the entire six years of the war. Such was the advance of science and military technology, that even before the advent of Hiroshima and Nagasaki, it was possible to kill 135,000 people in one night, as Kurt Vonnegut, who was present as an American war prisoner of the Germans, tells us happened in Dresden on 13 February 1945.

Here already, before we had gained entry to the epoch of nuclear weapons, war had evolved beyond the scope of Clausewitz' famous dictum. There is no sense in which carnage on this scale can be described as "a continuation of politics by other means". The politics so continued were now those of genocide. Henceforth war had left the domain of political action and entered that of crime.

American and British bombers unloaded 2.7 million tons of bombs in the European theatre of operations between October 1939 and May 1945. Sixty-one German cities were hit, and over three-and-a-half million homes destroyed. When they tried to evaluate the effects of this strategic bombing, immediately after hostilities had ceased, the Americans estimated that 300,000 civilians had been killed. This proved to be too low by half. But "although decline in morale was considerable" this "had practically no effect on armament production".[6] Air war could be "justified" as a terrorist expedient but not as a military instrument. Terror was not abandoned after 1945, however. During the three-year war in Korea, the North Koreans suffered half a million military casualties, and probably twice as many civilian ones. The bombardment was continuous and senseless. General O'Donnell, the head of Far Eastern Bomber Command, put it in a nutshell:

> "Everything is destroyed. There is nothing standing worthy of the name. Just before the Chinese came in we were grounded. There were no more targets in Korea."[7]

Pyongyang emerged from the war with only two of its buildings intact and only one-fifth of its population. Two thousand-plus bomber raids in 1952 were responsible for much of this destruction. The first unloaded more than 1,400 tons of bombs and 23,000 gallons of napalm. the second, an "all UN air effort", mobilised 1,405 bombers. Outside the cities, the systematic destruction of peasants by direct bombardment did not bring victory. Nor even did the deliberate assaults on irrigation dams, in spite of their horror. In May 1953, five of these dams were "taken out", and one of the resultant torrents "scooped clean 27 miles of valley".[8]

From Korea to Vietnam, terror simply grew and grew. In seven years, between 1965 and 1971, American military forces detonated 13 millions tons of high explosive in Indo-China, six-and-a-half millions tons of these from the air. "This staggering weight of ordnance amounts to the energy of 450 Hiroshima nuclear bombs. For the area and people of Indo-China as a whole it represents an average of 142 pounds of explosive per acre of land and 584 pounds per person . . . of the 26 billion pounds (13 million tons), 21 billions were exploded in South Vietnam . . . 497 pounds per acre and 1,215 pounds per person . . . craters pock every area of South Vietnam: forests, swamps, fields, paddies, roadsides . . ."[9] Even by 1971, Indo-China had absorbed a bombardment using twice the total of munitions employed by the United States in every zone in which it was embattled during the Second World War. "From the air some areas in Vietnam looked like photographs of the moon", said Westing and Pfeiffer in their mid-war scrutiny of the damage. The bombardment of Cambodia in 1972 and 1973 was no less systematic, even though it was illegally conducted, without the approval of Congress. Within 14 months, there were 3,630 B52 raids against Cambodia. A normal B52 mission included seven planes, and delivered 756 500-pound bombs to an area of almost 1,000 acres. All these figures inhibit comprehension. But they did not maintain America's chosen clients in Kampuchea. As William

Shawcross reported:

> "That summer's war provides a lasting image of peasant boys and girls, clad in black, moving slowly through the mud, half-crazed with terror as fighter-bombers tore down at them by day, and night after night whole seas of 750-pound bombs smashed all around. Week after week they edged forward, forever digging in, forever clambering slippery road banks to assault government outposts, forever losing comrades and going on in thinner ranks through a landscape that would have seemed lunar had it not been under water. They pushed towards the enemy's capital, urged on by their commanders, a small group of hardened zealous men who had lived up to 10 years in the isolation of the jungles, whose only experience of alliance was betrayal, whose only knowledge of war was massive retaliation."[10]

Crime bred crime. Trauma created trauma. The threat of US Air Force General Curtis LeMay was perfectly explicit:

> "My solution? Tell the Vietnamese they've got to draw in their horns and stop aggression or we're going to bomb them back into the Stone Age."

It can be argued that the secret war of President Nixon and Henry Kissinger against Cambodia did precisely that. And it was all accomplished with conventional weaponry. If one seeks a model for the behaviour of societies which have been subjected to nuclear bombardment, very probably our nearest actual approach to it can be found in the savage conflicts of Kampuchea, after this awesome orgy of destruction. The line between the effect of modern high explosive munitions and that of nuclear weapons is in this moral sense not quite so absolute as has been supposed, and there is available much testimony on this matter from the Third World, if we have ears to hear it.

If the classical socialist spokesmen had blinkers, this could be recognised in their approval (in the 19th century and beyond) of Clausewitz' old saw. There exists a Gresham's Law by which intellectual coin is debased, in which resounding slogans drive out profound sense. Surely Clausewitz has suffered from the money-clippers and reducers as much as anyone at the old Royal Mint. Today, everyone who hears his name will respond with the same catchphrase. But this has outworn any real meaning it might once have had. The roasting alive of Korean and Vietnamese children has not had much to do with any rational political process. Reason has been an early casualty in the technical over-reach of modern armourers.

A sure mark of barbarism is that so few of the people in the advanced world are aware of what has been happening in the outer darkness of colonial wars.

And yet we are still not lost . . . if we have not forgotten how to learn. What in fact has been learnt since the Second World War?

III: 'Imperialism' and Imperialisms

As I write, today's wars range around the world. A vast American Fleet has assembled in the Eastern Mediterranean and even President Reagan's closest and most taciturn ally has felt compelled to warn him from London against an attack on Syria. In another hemisphere, they are counting the bodies after the United States' occupation of Grenada. So far, the statistics are unofficial, but it has been alleged that many people have perished, the majority, of course, being non-combatants. In Afghanistan there is no sign of any let-up in the continuing slaughter. Nicaragua awaits further attack. Attacks there have already been, in large numbers, by mercenaries whose total dependence upon the Central Intelligence Agency no-one troubles to deny. CBS Television has even confirmed that those who sabotaged the Corinto fuel stores were ferried to the spot in speed boats driven by US military personnel. Tomorrow's war has already been seeded: for years now already battle has raged between Iran and Iraq, but at any moment the Americans are scheduled to intervene when the Straits of Hormuz are closed as will happen on the day that the first Exocet missile is fired against Iranian forces. There have already been some close calls.

All these bloody exchanges seem so predictable. Even so, there are grounds to disagree with Ernest Mandel, who tells us "Imperialism is more determined than ever to employ its counter-revolutionary violence against every revolutionary advance in the world. This takes the form of systematic armed intervention, sometimes disguised as support to one of the sides in a civil war, at other times an open massive foreign intervention".[11] Of American imperialism this is broadly true. But what of all the *other* imperialisms? Years ago, Mandel himself rightly insisted on their growing power and influence.[12] Now, by 1990 Japan will have larger overseas investments than the USA. How ironic it seems that this steady accumulation should continue while Americans discuss how Japan should rearm! If Western Europe is nowadays usually more pacific, has it become less imperialist? Links with Southern Africa are crucial to Britain; with South America, crucial to

Federal Germany. Yet, just as it was de Gaulle who presided over Algeria's Independence Day, it was Mrs Thatcher who was the midwife at the birth of Zimbabwe. How often do we hear responsible members of the German establishment offering their public regrets about the misbehaviour of the United States in its imperium, South of the Border? Are we, in short, no longer in an age of competing capitals? How can it be wise to speak of only one imperialism when the evidence of our eyes and ears repeatedly tells us of several? Here, for instance, is the reluctant testimony of one very committed partisan of the Atlantic Alliance, the Dutch scholar, Alting von Geusau, who heads the J.F. Kennedy Institute at Tilburg University in the Netherlands:

> "The current state of the alliance is not good. Allied policies are drifing apart, and outside events tend to exacerbate mutual relations instead of reuniting governments in their policies. Underlying these trends are forces at work that are likely to destroy the very fabric of allied cohesion. Among them are political polarisation, growing alienation between governments and their electorates, sharpening distrust and irritation among governments, and declining willingness to use the available instruments for effective, mutual consultation . . . a variety of economic issues (divide) the allies . . . Among them are rising protectionism in trade, European-American differences in monetary and fiscal policies, and diverging approaches to the problem of dependence on imported energy.
>
> It may be argued that trade between the United States and the EEC is less important a problem than investment and technological co-operation. With respect to energy dependence, Western Europe stresses improved political relations with OPEC and considers the gas pipeline deal with the Soviet Union as a welcome diversification of energy imports. Americans are seriously concerned about the impact this deal may have on West European security. As far as Middle East oil is concerned, Americans tend to emphasise the need for an ability to protect the flow of oil against eventual Soviet attempts to disrupt it . . . the competing interests and divergent approaches . . . to relations with developing countries . . . are peripheral rather than central to the problem of maintaining allied cohesions in the 1980s. Still, the impact that economic divergences could have on allied cohesion should not be under-estimated."[13]

Since this assessment was published, long ago in 1982, "allied cohesion" has been diminishing month by month. Perhaps the ties established in the late 1940s will hold a little longer. Perhaps not. It is already necessary for socialists to begin to table for discussion the burning question, "after the Atlantic Alliance, what next?" Certainly this is a more reasonable question than von Geusau's hope that "the main democratic political parties will" respect the limits to be observed in "support for the Alliance and for the political order for which it stands". While the peace movements express overwhelming resentment of Alliance nuclear policy, President Reagan systematically bruises the shins of each ally in turn, as he asserts the primacy of American interests over all. Up to now, it is true that the inter-imperial disputes have been in large measure contained within the alliance framework: but each of these conflicts has strained that framework a little bit more, and its structure now looks anything but solid. We need to remember this when we examine Ernest Mandel's main argument.

He offers us a long catalogue of imperial wars. Rightly, he draws attention to the significance of the Rapid Deployment Force as a new imperial defence mechanism. This, however, is not an isolated phenomenon. It is linked with the forward deployment of Pershing II missiles in Federal Germany, the installation of cruise missiles over the entire arc of Western Europe, the doctrine of "Airland Battle", and the overall preparation of war fighting rather than responding deterrence. When he goes on to tell us that colonial repressions represent "a return to 'the norm': that is, the systematic obstinate attempt of imperialism to pit its counter-revolutionary strength against each new advance of revolution",[14] Mandel insists that this "norm" is not in the least a new phenomenon, and does not imply an imminent outbreak of world war.[15] True, he concedes "an element of truth" in the possibility that the danger of nuclear war might increase with increasing nuclear arsenals and the multiplication of local conflicts. But he does not confront, and nowhere recognises the possibility, that such colonial conflicts might "spill back" into superpower conflicts in the manner described by, say, Alva Myrdal.[16] Each linkage in United States' military policy makes this more likely, so that it is already highly probable. Neither does Mandel perceive the possibility that the very frailty of the Alliance might provoke conflict about this, up to the point at which its constituents can formally separate. The fact is that since 1945 there has been a succession of colonial wars in which liberation movements have been confronted by a variety of imperialisms, most of which, most of the time, have been in greater or lesser solidarity one with another. Not all of these conflicts have been "imperialist" in the economic sense of the term. What we have *not* had, in the sense that classic socialist writers conceived it, is *imperialist* war, war between contending empires, or between those aspiring to empire and those defending its possession. As competition between major centres of capitalism increases, there is less and less reason why such centres should cohere in joint policies or respect each other's extended trading zones, leave alone residual spheres of influence.

IV: The Role of Labour in Preventing War

Mandel tells us that he believes that the upsurge of colonial struggles coincides with "up-turns in the global strength of the Labour movement". He believes that world war is unlikely to break out while this movement remains strong. In support of this proposition, the only evidence which he offers seems distinctly thin. Did not both previous world wars break out, he asks us, after either "a sudden breakdown in Labour militancy", or "after a long chain of defeats" for workers?[17] But these questions must surely provoke others: what constituted the "sudden breakdown" in 1914? Why, what but the outbreak of war? Certainly industrial militancy generally fell off in the year 1915 when mobilisation was rushing men towards the front for mass butchery. But in more than one country, and in many industries, the Labour unrest which marked the years 1911, 1912 and 1913 was continuing with great vigour right up to the moment of the outbreak of war. In Britain, the level of strike activity remained intense. Trade union membership continued to climb past the four million mark, while the proportion of intransigent strikes lasting for more than one month reached almost one quarter of the total. Similarly in Russia, as Trotsky showed in the early pages of his *History of the Russian Revolution,* strikes for political reasons reached an amazing peak in the first half of 1914. Beyond doubt, the outbreak of war arrested this trend: but it is not serious to argue that the war was caused or even facilitated, because industrial discontent was *about* to diminish. No. This unrest was transmuted into a frenzy of national bloodlust, which was itself one of the greatest ordeals ever undergone by international socialism. No-one has evoked its sulphurous atmosphere better than Trotsky, again:

> "At the first sound of the drum the revolutionary movement died down. The more active layers of the workers were mobilised. The revolutionary elements were thrown from the factories to the front. Severe penalties were imposed for striking. The workers' press was swept away. Trade unions were strangled. Hundreds of thousands of women, boys, peasants, poured into the workshops. The war — combined with the wreck of the International — greatly disoriented the workers politically, and made it possible for the factory administration, then just lifting its head, to speak patriotically in the name of the factories, carrying with it a considerable part of the workers, and compelling the more bold and

resolute to keep still and wait. The revolutionary ideas were barely kept glowing in small and hushed circles. In the factories in those days nobody dared to call himself 'Bolshevik' for fear not only of arrest, but of a beating from the backward workers."[18]

In England Bertrand Russell would not have dreamed of calling himself a Bolshevik, but that did not stop him from being attacked by patriots armed with boards studded with rusty nails. "Save him," a bystander told the police, "he is an eminent philosopher". No constable moved. "He is famous all over the world as a man of learning", insisted his would-be rescuer. Still no-one moved. "But he is the brother of an Earl" she finally cried. "At this", he later wrote, "the police rushed to my assistance". Pacifist workers were likely to be less fortunate.

In this respect, the Second World War differed markedly from the first. By contrast with the decade of syndicalism and socialist growth before 1914, 1939 came after the victory of Fascism in a number of countries, and no-one will doubt that this weakened the Labour movement almost everywhere in Europe. However, in the USA, labour militancy reached a peak and effectiveness never since paralleled.

In reality, Mandel has two different cases to deal with. Labour combativity was rising in the first, up to 1914; while the trade union and Labour movements were commonly suffering defeats (amounting sometimes to their total destruction) in the second, before 1939. From such evidence it might be thought rather difficult to generalise about the precise state of labour relations around the world which might or might not conduce to the outbreak of a third world war. We should be better advised to attend to other evidence, in the hope of a more comprehensive and plausible explanation. Apart from anything else, the run-up to the next great war sees the Peace movement gathering unprecedented strength, whilst in one country after another, Labour suffers major electoral defeats and trade unions are haunted by the grotesque rise in unemployment.

Although there were important differences between them, both of Mandel's instances concerned wars which began between imperial powers, not a confrontation between a rickety imperial "alliance" on the one side, and a tensely fractious group of states describing themselves as "socialist" on the other. Much as (or little as) we pay attention to noisy ideological arguments, might we not be forgiven for fearing that the competition between capitals could still tend to secrete wars? If the plurality of "socialisms" continues, is it impossible that some of these might find themselves drawn into different orbits around, perhaps, Japan or close, maybe, to Germany?

However, shaky though they may be, two alliances do now confront one another, and two major nuclear powers steel this confrontation. More: the problem about the development of nuclear weapons technology is that it renders decisions about whether or not to levy war greatly more unaccountable and therefore uncontrollable than they have ever been in previous history. And in affirming this reality, we are not claiming that wars have normally been launched by due democratic process. The contrary is true. The Labour movements of the warring powers in Europe failed to stop the First World War, and this was undoubtedly a major disaster for both democracy and socialism, the ill-effects of which survive even as we approach the last decade of the century. But it was not at all impossible in principle for mass organisations to resist a drift to a type of war which was scheduled to involve the movements of vast forces of infantry, armed with rifles, machine guns and high explosives. Even after the outbreak of war, at least in theory such great armies could be disaffected by socialist propaganda. In one case, they actually were. For all that, the Socialist International had an overall programme for resisting the onset of war, and it was that programme which collapsed in the face of the challenge it was designed to meet. This event was large enough to fracture world socialism for seven decades and we shall return to it later. Today, by contrast with the age of universal mobilisation, war has become a fearfully capital intensive business. Once nuclear weapons have been deployed, the initiative, and still more the execution, is held in far fewer hands than have ever held it hitherto.

V: 'Using' and Opposing Nuclear Weapons

Mandel offers us only one solid reason for hoping that a nuclear war will not break out, and that reason is that "those who possess nuclear weapons and can decide whether to use them know perfectly well their suicidal meaning for humanity". There is some evidence for this proposition. We have already referred to the remarkable statement of Lord Mountbatten, who was for long at the centre of British military affairs. It provides a notable confirming instance,

"As a militaryman who has given half a century of active Service I say in all sincerity that the nuclear arms race has no military purpose. Wars cannot be fought with nuclear weapons. Their existence only adds to our perils because of the illusions which they have generated.

There are powerful voices around the world who still give credence to the old Roman precept — if you desire peace, prepare for war. This is absolute nuclear nonsense and I repeat — it is a disastrous misconception to believe that by increasing the total uncertainty one increases one's own certainty.''[19]

But Mountbatten's protest was, as we have already insisted, concerned with the danger of the doctrine of limited nuclear war, and it was not directed against figments of his imagination. Let us recall his warning:

"Because of the enormous amount of destruction that could be wreaked by a single nuclear explosion, the idea was that both sides in what we still see as an East-West conflict would be deterred from taking any aggressive action which might endanger the vital interests of the other.

It was not long, however, before smaller nuclear weapons of various designs were produced and deployed for use in what was assumed to be a tactical or theatre war. The belief was that were hostilities ever to break out in Western Europe, such weapons could be used in field warfare without triggering an all-out nuclear exchange leading to the final holocaust.

I have never found this idea credible. I have never been able to accept the reasons for the belief that any class of nuclear weapons can be categorised in terms of their tactical or strategic purposes.''[20]

Mountbatten had lost his argument within the Western establishment and the present new escalation in the arms race is the outcome of this fact. Cruise and Pershing II missiles are being deployed in order to close a missing rung in the "ladder of escalation" which is part of the basic NATO strategic concept of limited nuclear war, albeit a policy rightly opposed by Britain's former Chief of the Imperial General Staff.[21] Mountbatten and his friend Lord Zuckerman have, as we have seen, given very eloquent arguments in favour of a "deterrent" use for nuclear weapons rather than a war-fighting use for them. But since they lost the argument inside NATO's hierarchy, so, too, has Mandel outside that forum. Present NATO doctrine locks the alliance in a pattern of response which will inevitably unleash nuclear weapons at an early stage in the development of any over-arching conflict. Does not this decision itself bear any relation to the outcome of a struggle between economic interests?

The development of nuclear conflict surely becomes more, not less likely with the attainment of broad Soviet parity in the nuclear arms race. Indeed, the messages which have been coming from the Soviet leadership indicate that they do not intend to flinch in pursuing this arms race and they will match NATO capacity item for item. This means that the Soviet leadership, also, are not accumulating weapons purely for defensive "deterrence", which could be bought far cheaper. An adequate threshold of nuclear weaponry to deter aggression would be rather low. The possession of perhaps 7½ thousand strategic warheads and probably 10 thousand or more allegedly "tactical" ones has not made defensive deterrence one whit more credible than an arsenal a tenth or a twentieth of that size.

It is thus quite remarkable that Mandel can claim that "The fact that the Soviet Union has built and stockpiled nuclear weapons has saved humanity up till now from a nuclear holocaust. Without this 'balance of terror' it is practically certain that imperialism would already have used nuclear weapons against the "Chinese volunteers" during the Korean war, against the Indo-Chinese revolutions during the second Indo-Chinese war, and, indeed, against other revolutions."[22]

The first thing to say about this remarkable judgement is that it flatly contradicts Mandel's earlier statement that "despite the development of an ever more terrifying arsenal of nuclear weapons over the last 30 years, they *have not been used* until now".[23] (My emphasis). There is more than one use for an atom bomb. If for a moment, for the sake of argument, we concede that it was only the existence of Soviet nuclear armament which deterred United States nuclear bombardments in the cases instanced, then the weapons *have* been used, first by the Americans to threaten, then by the Russians to counter such threats. If I point a pistol at Mandel and invite him to part with his wallet, am I or am I not "using" the pistol? In fact, the Americans have in this sense "used" the nuclear pistol on many occasions.

Milton Leitenberg has collected the evidence documenting many of these uses, together with a number of other nuclear warnings which have been uttered by the Soviet Union. He offers us a typology of four distinct categories of such events.[24] First, there is the rather generalised threat involved in overall deployment, such as is involved in the decision to install Cruise and Pershing missiles in Western Europe, or the Soviet deployment of theatre nuclear forces along the Chinese frontier. Secondly, there are precise verbal threats to employ nuclear weapons, such as those made by the Soviet Union in 1956 at the time of the French and British involvement in the Suez crisis.[25] These took the shape of "diplomatic messages delivered to a head of state". Thirdly, there are decisions to move to increased alert levels of nuclear weapon systems, whether these are publicly announced or not. A notable instance of such an action was the unilateral decision of the United States Government to put all American military commands throughout the world on standby, during the Middle East crisis of October 1973. This state of readiness, known as Defcon III, involves the most complete general deployment of nuclear weapons, and its seriousness cannot easily be over-stated. We shall discuss this particular instance later, in another context. Fourthly, there are specific deployments of nuclear weapon systems during a particular crisis.

According to Leitenberg, the second category of warning action, involving verbal threats, has been most frequently used by the Soviet Union. The third category, of public nuclear alerts, has so far been a monopoly of the United States. Two of these have been the subject of an extensive literature: but there are, says Leitenberg, "many more situations of increased alert levels than the public knows about". As for specific deployments, Leitenberg estimates there may have been "about a hundred" of these since the middle 1950s, when the United States Fleet began to deploy nuclear weapons on its aircraft carriers.

Table 1

Incidents in which US Strategic Nuclear Forces were Involved

US aircraft shot down by Yugoslavia	November 1946
Inauguration of President in Uruguay	February 1947
Security of Berlin	January 1948
Security of Berlin	April 1948
Security of Berlin	June 1948
Korean War: Security of Europe	July 1950
Security of Japan/South Korea	August 1953
Guatemala accepts Soviet bloc support	May 1954
China-Taiwan conflict: Tachen Islands	August 1954
Suez crisis	October 1956
Political crisis in Lebanon	July 1958
Political crisis in Jordan	July 1958
China-Taiwan crisis: Quemoy and Matsu	July 1958
Security of Berlin	May 1959
Security of Berlin	June 1961
Soviet emplacement of missiles in Cuba	October 1962
Withdrawal of US missiles from Turkey	April 1963
Pueblo seized by North Korea	January 1968
Arab-Israeli War	October 1973

Blechman and Kaplan furnish a list of 19 important incidents in which American strategic nuclear forces have been involved.[26] These are tabulated in Table 1. Leitenberg argues that some of these must be considered separately, as self-evidently more serious than the others. Of course, one threat may provoke another, and Leitenberg has traced reports of up to a dozen cases in which Soviet verbal nuclear threats have been issued, some of which constituted responses to other categories of threat from the United States.

"We have been fortunate" says this author "that this level of use has not led to actual use in wartime, but that has perhaps been due to more complex factors than the restraint with which we ordinarily assume nuclear weapons are handled".[27]

Mandel is particularly concerned with American initiatives, and it is instructive to follow him on to this ground. Daniel Ellsberg has discussed some of these threats[28] starting in 1946, only seven months after the nuclear bombardment of Nagasaki. President Truman is alleged to have summoned Soviet Ambassador Gromyko and invited him to evacuate Iran within 48 hours "or the US would use the new super-bomb that it alone possessed. 'We are going to drop it on you', Senator Jackson quoted Truman as saying . . . 'They moved in 24 hours'." If this story has not been unambiguously confirmed, many other actual nuclear crises have.

In June 1948, B29s were sent to bases in Britain and Germany at the beginning of the Berlin blockade. On 30 November 1950, Truman gave a warning at a press conference that he was considering using nuclear weapons threats against China, information about which is to be found in the first volume of his memoirs *Mandate for Change*: "In order to compel the Chinese Communists to accede to an armistice, it was obvious that if we were to go over to a major offensive the war would have to be expanded outside of Korea — with strikes against the supporting Chinese airforce in Manchuria, a blockade of the Chinese coast and similar measures . . . Finally, to keep the attack from becoming overtly costly, it was clear that we would have to use atomic weapons . . . We dropped the word, discreetly, of our intention".[29] A further secret offer was made to Premier Bidault of France, in 1954, at the time of the siege of Dien Bien Phu. French troops were surrounded, and the American Secretary of State, Foster Dulles, was willing to make available three tactical nuclear bombs to prevent their defeat. Mendes France reported this offer in a speech he made in the National Assembly on 10 June 1954. There were similar direct threats, reports Ellsberg, during the Lebanon crisis of

1958, the Quemoy crisis of 1958, the Berlin Crisis of 1961, the Cuban missile crisis of 1962, the Khe Sanh battle of Vietnam in 1968, again in Vietnam during the Nixon years between 1969-72, and more recently in the Middle East. Each of these was a "use" of nuclear weapons, although these uses were not equally successful. However, if we examine those cases in which such threats failed, there is no clearly established case in which failure can be attributed to the deterrent effect of Soviet nuclear weapons. Normally, it is plain that these have had nothing to do with the outcome. A possible exception to this judgement might be made in the crisis over Quemoy in 1958.

Edgar Snow offers a revealing discussion of this episode, in which President Eisenhower sent the 7th Fleet to the Taiwan Strait, and announced that the American airforce had been equipped with nuclear missiles, in order to prevent the possibility of a Chinese landing on the Island of Quemoy.[30] The Eisenhower mobilisation cost a billion dollars, and interdicted an occupation which was almost certainly never contemplated, but there can be no doubt that it provoked serious discussions between the Chinese and Soviet Governments, since it put in question the value of the Soviet "nuclear umbrella". Franz Schurmann thinks that the Chinese found this umbrella "somewhat reassuring", and he might agree with Mandel that the United States was in fact deterred by fear of Soviet nuclear weapons during that confrontation.[31]

But further, Edgar Snow points out with some irony, that the American ultimatum did maintain the right of the forces of Chiang Kai Shek to molest Chinese shipping, "umbrella" notwithstanding. This gives rise to a complex question. When superpowers are gaming over a particular territory, it is not always easy to adjudicate the precise effect of their threats and counter-threats. That the United States did not in fact attack China in 1958 is true, but that the Chinese were unable to assert their rightful control over their own territorial waters is also true. Thus those who say that the Americans were deterred by the fear of Soviet nuclear reprisals can make a case of a kind, although hardly an impregnable one.

Over a large part of this period, the strategic advantage ran so heavily in favour of the Americans that it is not serious to speak of a Soviet deterrent, leave alone the capacity of the Soviet Union to "save humanity from . . . holocaust" by threatening holocaust.

Both during the 1946 Iran crisis, when the Russians had not yet detonated their first trial fission device, and later, during the 1962

Cuba crisis, when the Soviet Union was way behind the Americans in intercontinental strike capacity, Russian retreats were, it seems quite incontestable, a necessary capitulation to superior strength. In this negative sense, of course, "deterrence" theory is valid, and the increase of Soviet nuclear capacity undoubtedly rendered such capitulation unnecessary in the future. I have discussed this question earlier in Chapter 1. As between the two great nuclear powers, nuclear weapons have provided a powerful incentive for each to stand off from the other. The snag in this process is that it involves a runaway arms race, in which quantitative build-up is increasingly likely to create a new qualitative relationship, as technologies increase the uncertainty of the tottering balance of force.

But in all the cases actually cited by Mandel, it was demonstrably not "the balance of terror" but the force of public opinion taken together with differences in the State interests of Alliance members, which prevented the explosion of nuclear weapons once the threat to use them had been uttered. In the case of China, during the Korean war, President Truman's November 1950 threat to use atomic bombs in the Korean war provoked an instant response throughout the world. In England, 100 MPs signed a letter to Attlee urging the British Labour Government to dissociate Britain from the use of the atomic bomb, to refuse any action outside the decisions of the United Nations and to warn that any unilateral action would be followed by the withdrawal of British forces from Korea. A fraught debate followed in the House of Commons, and the concern spilt over into the Conservative Party. Truman's memoirs record that the United States Embassy relayed the concern of Churchill, Eden and Butler "that events in Korea would not propel the world into a major war'.[32] At this point, Attlee flew to Washington for a personal conference with Truman. Nuclear weapons were not detonated. Following this confrontation, there developed a considerable split in the British Labour Party and Aneurin Bevan carried forward a truly remarkable campaign to organise solidarity with the Chinese revolution, the recognition of Peoples' China by the United Nations, and the establishment of normal relations with the new Chinese Government. Even after the Labour Party had been defeated in the British General Election of 1951, this campaign continued to mobilise opinion, and was undoubtedly an influence during the second phase of nuclear intimidation towards the end of the Korean war.

When we come to examine the intention to bombard the beseigers of Dien Bien Phu, we have the words of Mendes France for it: "The United States intervention was to have taken place on the request of France, April 28. The three ships carrying atomic aviation material were loaded and en route. President Eisenhower . . . was to have asked Congress . . . for authorisation. Luckily the project of the US intervention was set aside by Britain and public opinion in the United States".[33]

In none of these cases was the Soviet military capacity adequate to respond on any significant scale. The imbalance in nuclear power was such that the American Government could quite easily have risked fulfilling its threat, had it been prepared to confront the consequent disarray with its alliances, and the resultant cost in domestic unpopularity. Since the 1960s, nuclear armaments in the USSR have become numerous and are a prodigious power. Are they, then, a "deterrent" of any use in the developing struggle for colonial freedom? We must surely doubt this. The Soviet Union also suffers from the inverse logic so coherently described by Henry Kissinger in the late 1950s: it cannot deploy its force unless it is willing to risk its own destruction.

"Given the power of modern weapons", wrote Kissinger in 1957, "a nation that relies on all-out war imposes a fearful psychological handicap on itself . . . As the power of modern weapons grows, the threat of all-out war loses its credibility and therefore its political effectiveness. Our capacity for massive retaliation did not avert the Korean war, the loss of Northern Indo-China, the Soviet-Egyptian arms deal, or the Suez crisis. Moreover, whatever the credibility of our threat of all-out war, it is clear that all-out thermo-nuclear war does not represent a strategic option for our allies. Thus a psychological gap is created by the conviction of our allies that they have nothing to gain from massive retaliation and by the belief of the Soviet leaders that the have nothing to fear from our threat of it."[34]

Does this not perfectly describe the dilemma confronting the Soviet Government in its relations with China during the period of repeated American nuclear threats against China? And were the Chinese wrong to doubt that a Soviet Government might risk the certain annihilation of the USSR by retaliating against any American nuclear strike on Chinese cities? Allies may have high expectations one of another: they may anticipate reciprocal sacrifices. But an alliance which could withstand this kind of pressure would be a suicide pact. For this reason, all the vast accumulation of nuclear power is, for most practical purposes, impotent. Nobody will expect the Soviet nuclear umbrella to protect Nicaragua, any more than Grenada. Even in Syria, so much closer to home, the Soviets will not readily invoke the possible use of nuclear weapons. When it is examined, in all the long list of colonial struggles itemised by Mandel, there is not one unambiguous example of a case in which the Soviet possession of nuclear weapons has really made the decisive difference.

There is, however, one major recorded example of a *Soviet* nuclear threat, and it is in a much less edifying cause that those which have been listed by Mandel.

Apparently, after the Sino-Soviet clashes in 1969, the Soviet Union began to put systematic pressure on China to settle the border dispute. This pressure had already involved the use of direct military force but in the autumn the Soviet leaders decided to augment it by allowing it to be known that they were contemplating a nuclear strike against China.

This threat was issued as the culmination of a military build-up on Chinese borders which came to a head in the winter of 1968-69 with armed clashes on the Ussuri Island of Chenpao or Damansky. Soon afterwards there were a series of reports in the Western press[35] that the Soviet Government had threatened to launch a nuclear strike against Chinese atomic bases, unless the Chinese agreed to talks which could sort out this border problem. The military build-up continued to escalate through the early 1970s, but talks did take place, from 1969 on. Indeed we now have rather complete evidence of the circumstances which gave rise to this. On 11 September 1969, Premier Chou en Lai met with Premier Kosygin in Beijing. After his disagreement with the Chinese became public, the Albanian leader Enver Hoxha published his political diary, which contains an angry record of his shock at this unexpected meeting. The Chinese had not informed the Albanians in advance, but the Albanian Ambassador in Peking subsequently cabled his Government with the information that the talks were about the settlement of the border problems, problems of communication and trade, and the exchange of Ambassadors. The Chinese made two preconditions for participating in these talks: one was that the ideological controversy would continue, and the other "The Chinese atomic bases must not be attacked by the Soviets because then it would be all-out war". Hoxha's diary gives his reaction to this: "The Americans spread a 'sensational' report: the Soviet Union is going to attack China and especially the Chinese atomic bases. The bourgeois press and chancelleries continued to inflate this report. The bloody Soviet provocations on the Chinese border and the massing of hundreds of thousands of Soviet troops over the whole length of the Sino-Soviet border, support this report.

Can the Soviet revisionists have taken such a decision? Anything is possible, but I think that this is a Soviet-American bluff to intimidate China''.[36] Hoxha believed that Soviet internal divisions were sufficiently acute to prevent the actual launching of war, but "in my opinion, the Chinese were terrified and wavered in the face of this colossal blackmail frame up''. Hoxha believed that Chou en Lai might have exploited the Soviet threat[37] in order to seize the pretext for beginning talks. Later, the Albanian Ambassador in Beijing criticised the meeting with Kosygin and was in turn rebuked as an extremist by Premier Chou. This provoked an extensive entry in Hoxha's diary, discussing the alleged perfidy of his Chinese comrades in running scared of the Soviet threat. This he discusses as "bluff and blackmail", "strengthening revisionists and undermining the cultural revolution".[38] By October, Hoxha was still communicating with his diary in the same vein. In the same way that the threat of a nuclear strike "worked" when Truman made it to Gromyko, so it "worked" again in China. Not only were negotiations resumed, however. The Chinese also developed a feverish campaign for the construction of nuclear shelters in all their major cities. Throughout the early 1970s, a vast tunnel system was created in Beijing and other towns.

When I was there in April 1983, these enormous underground retreats had been opened, where possible, to civilian uses. Some idea of their scale can be obtained from listing these. There are four dining rooms in the vast Dongtian restaurant, with a service area of 1,000 square metres. A 320-bedroom hotel has been created in another part of the labyrinth. Altogether, Beijing now has some 100 such underground hotels. It also has an immense department store with a 5,000-metre nuclear shelter basement, 24,000 square metres of fruit depository, rifle ranges, a roller-skating rink for 900 people, theatres, underground meeting halls, clinics, libraries and a gymnasium.[39]

Although socialists may have their preferences (on different scales) for these and those social political relationships which exist in the USSR or China, there can be no doubt that the nuclear threat against China involved its vast outlay of scarce material resources. This must have been hard to bear in a country which has been desperately seeking the means of exit from under-development.

True, one of the foremost British experts on Soviet military power, David Holloway, tells us "there is no evidence to suggest that (the USSR) were seriously contemplating a nuclear attack, that this was more than an attempt at intimidation".[40] But intimidation which can redirect vitally precious economic resources on so huge a scale is by no means a negligible event. And even today, now that there are welcome signs of the beginning of a Sino-Soviet detente, there are still between 117 and 126 Soviet SS20s deployed along the Chinese frontier, (depending on whether one controversial site is in fact operational or not). Each of these missiles carries three warheads, so that a minimum of 351 warheads are targeted on 40 million Chinese Communists and one billion of the world's poorest but most organised people, whose success in the struggle for economic development may be said to be entirely crucial for the future of the world. It is not easy to see how Soviet nuclear weapons benefit these people, or how placing them under nuclear threat can benefit the Soviet peoples themselves. How many potential Hiroshimas are necessary to fortify this communist frontier?

VI: The Superpowers and Exterminism

Soviet protagonists in the debate about nuclear weapons are frequently at pains to insist that the concept of "superpower" is misleading, and that we should really see the world conflict as a great international class struggle. Ernest Mandel seems to be echoing this kind of response, even though he would never advocate the use of nuclear weapons in defence of even the most beleaguered outpost of the colonial revolution. But surely he must see that the Soviet leadership deprive themselves of this argument by deploying such enormous nuclear forces against Communist China? It is not enough to say what is perfectly evident, that the Chinese have no conceivable capacity with which to launch aggressive war against the USSR: even if this were not so, socialists would surely be wise to insist upon a categorical imperative that disputes between states proclaiming adherence to socialism must be solved without recourse to violence of any kind, leave alone the ultimate obscenity of nuclear violence. Naturally this insistence would extend to Chinese relations with Vietnam, and Vietnamese relations with Cambodia. It would apply in Central Europe and the Balkans also. It constitutes a general prescription, not a conditional or factional commitment.

Disarmament of and between the two great nuclear powers, by contrast, could only be accomplished as a result of vast social pressure by nations and peace movements all around the world, and even in the best case, it would necessarily involve a bilateral process of agreement. Mr Andropov has sternly informed us that the Soviet Union will not accept the idea of unilateral disarmament. But, from any socialist or communist viewpoint, if there is one zone in which the Soviets should be expected to disarm unilaterally, it is along this Chinese frontier. All these SS20s could be dismantled, without respect to any other disagreements which might exist between China and the USSR. This would be the most powerful proof that the arms race should not be considered "symmetrical", that the superpowers do not simply reflect each other's military structures, and that the Soviet leadership was willing to take active steps to liquidate all those tendencies in its behaviour which have been described by critics as hegemonistic.

However, even if such a benevolent gesture is not forthcoming, and it is prudent to admit that it may not be, the maintenance of this confrontation will not demonstrate that the sociology of nuclear collision, or of nuclear deterrence for the matter, rests upon "similar", "symmetrical" or "identical" bases. Even "convergence" would remain unproven. This issue has been widely discussed since Edward Thompson addressed himself to it, and this has not prevented some considerable misrepresentation of his view.

Mandel offers some valid comments on Edward Thompson's important paper on Exterminism.[41] Thompson is a brilliant journalist, and his writing illuminates by a process of suggestive metaphor rather than analytic rigour. This does not invalidate what he has to say, even when his message is overlaid with pessimism. There are precedents for pessimism.

Indeed, in the present age of nuclear weapons, pessimism seems to many people to be the most rational stance. Herbert Marcuse, for instance: "Intensified progress seems to be bound up with intensified unfreedom. Throughout the world of industrial civilisation, the domination of man by man is growing in scope and efficiency. In our days, this trend appears as an incidental, transitory regression on the road to progress. Concentration camps, mass exterminations, world wars, and atom bombs, are no 'relapse into barbarism', but the unrepressed implementation of the achievements of modern science, technology and domination. And the most effective subjugation and destruction of man by man takes place at the height of civilisation, when the material and intellectual attainments of man seem to allow the creation of a truly free world".[42]

It was this kind of understanding which provoked Edward Thompson to ask, "If 'the hand-mill gives you society with the feudal lord; the steam-mill, society with the industrial capitalist' what are we given by those satanic-mills which are now at work, grinding out the means of human extermination? I have reached this point of thought more than once before, but have turned my head away in despair. Now, when I look at it directly I know that the category which we need is that of 'exterminism'."[43]

Thompson is right that the military organisation of the modern world is a live and growing social phenomenon. Speaking with irony, he parodies the Left by saying "As for the bomb, that is a Thing and a Thing cannot be a historical agent".[44] But an important part of the Left has known for a very long time that things may affect social agencies. The mechanical production lines associated with Fordism, for instance, were accurately identified by Gramsci, and again by such writers as Mallet and Goldmann, as developing an associated consciousness which had direct results on the agencies of social change. Bertrand Russell, who was well-known to be agnostic about many of the principles of Marxism, insisted almost 50 years ago that:

> "Changes in the technique of war have had more influence upon the course of history than is supposed by those whose attention is mainly centred upon economic causation. There has been, since the beginning of organised fighting, an oscillation between superiority of the defensive and superiority of the offensive. Broadly speaking, when the defensive is strong civilisation makes progress, and when the offensive is strong men revert towards barbarism. Another oscillation has been between the importance of mere numbers and the importance of skill and elaborate equipment. In the Middle Ages, the knight in armour was an expensive unit, and the world was aristocratic; gunpowder abolished chivalry, and led by slow stages to citizen armies and democracy."[45]

Of course, military expenditure has reached such phenomenal levels that all social organisation is grossly distorted through the iron mesh which extrudes the society of militarism. World military expenditures run at more than 19,000 dollars per soldier, compared to less than 400 dollars educational expenditure per school age child; there are more than 550 soldiers in every 100,000 people, but the same population enjoys the ministrations of only 85 physicians.[46] World military expenditures have risen from $503bn in 1975 to $532bn dollars three years later, and $561bn at the beginning of this decade. They are scheduled to continue to rise and they have indeed already passed $618bn per annum.[47] These statistics are the monetary reflections of vast human organisations, each one of which has imposed its own pattern of debility on the community structures of the society which supports it.

In 1982, the United States had something over 10,000 strategic nuclear warheads and the USSR about 7,400. (In 1962, at the time when Khrushchev "blinked" in the Cuba crisis, the balance of strategic warheads had been 70 in the USSR and 2,000 in the USA). The present balance of tactical nuclear weaponry is even more awe-inspiring: especially when one considers that the weapons styled "tactical" are commonly considerably more powerful than the bombs which devastated Hiroshima and Nagasaki in 1945. The United States apparently deploys some 20,000 such tactical weapons against 10,000 Soviet weapons.

If we are looking for evidence of barbarism, it is already to hand: even before the outbreak of nuclear war, this vast procurement of nuclear weapons is correlated with economic decline, rising unemployment, and growing starvation in the poorest countries of the world. At the beginning of the decade the OECD estimated that world-wide economic aid was running at $36bn, or greatly less than a tithe of the world military budget in 1980. Meantime, perhaps a billion people live on the verge of starvation.

For all these reasons, Edward Thompson is right to deny that the bomb may be dismissed as simply a "thing". Around the structures which deploy the bomb are determined social divisions of labour into which fit those who make, develop and deploy it. Once established this must needs affect the continued evolution of the overall division of labour. At this point, however, Thompson moves his argument forward: "No doubt we will have one day a comprehensive analysis of the origins of the cold war, in which the motives of the agents appear as rational. But that cold war passed, long ago, into a self-generating condition of cold-warism (exterminism) in which the originating drives, reactions and intentions are still at play, but within a general inertial condition . . ." Such a process, Thompson reasons, has left the plane of rationality, not because individual leaders are insane, (although sometimes they are) but because there exists this "inertial thrust" towards war, drawing its force from the deep structured militarisation of the contending societies. "The USA and the USSR do not *have* military industrial complexes: they *are* such complexes."[48]

As we have said, the nuclear armaments of these powers have, since 1962, moved very much closer to parity. The conventional wisdom in the West, when Mr Khrushchev turned aside from the naval confrontation with which Kennedy responded to the initial deployment of missiles in Cuba, was that the theory of deterrence had been justified. At one level, this theory embodies a truism, so that Khrushchev's decision to turn back was hardly surprising, when he faced such overwhelmingly disproportionate strength. But as competent practitioners of the same theory of deterrence, Khrushchev's colleagues drew all the requisite lessons in order to avoid a repetition of such humiliation.[49] The hundredfold development of their strategic nuclear arsenals in the following years is, to be sure, evidence of an insane competition, but it is unfortunately not "irrational", but entirely "normal" within the rules of that game. Of course, all of us would desire that things were different, and that the arms race were being run in the opposite direction, towards the dismantling of all nuclear weapons. To outlaw the game would be sensible: to incarcerate the players is beyond anyone's powers, so we have no option but to develop rational pressures towards a world order which does not engender such follies.

It is in the light of this need that we must evaluate Thompson's assessment that "the USA and the USSR do not *have* military industrial complexes: they *are* such complexes". These formations, he concedes, have a "leading sector" of weapons systems and supports, which, protected by official secrecy, enjoy "low visibility". Speaking in such terms may indeed have been justified while such low visibility was the rule, because the metaphor served to warn of the existence of a great menace. But in sobriety, now that we are able to hear the voices of millions of peace marchers, we are bound to see some exaggeration in this warning formula.

At one level this exaggeration has been adequately chronicled by Zhores and Roy Medvedev in their response to the *Exterminism* article.[50]

The Soviet complex, they say, is not a "state within a state", but a subordinate state unit. On the other side, competition between services, as well as transnational corporations, ensures that the military-industrial complex in the USA retains a sinister, inverted pluralism, which continuously generates "overproduction" of arms systems. Perhaps as seriously, competition between Western exporters of civilian nuclear installations increases the trend to military nuclear proliferation: a trend which has been stolidly resisted by the Soviet administration, but abetted, not only by private contractors, but also by actual States in the West.

None of this is to deny the scale of the Soviet input to war preparation: starting as it does from a lower civilian basis, it preempts a far larger proportion of Gross National Product than is required to maintain the vast American output of weaponry. Amongst the resources it gobbles up, we can hardly overlook the precious human skills, which may well mean that many of the most talented, creative people find their way into the military sectors. To the extent that they do, their advocacy will serve to skew development still further. The Soviet system finds these resources, presumably with difficulty, by central command out of a planned economy. The feel of this process has been clearly described by an American journalist, Robert Kaiser, who spent three years in the USSR on behalf of the *Washington Post:*

> "The military economy is not apart from the rest; it is the cream on top of the rest. Its accomplishments are the ultimate tribute to the music school approach to the allocation of resources. The military economy gets the most resources and makes the best products.
>
> To a great extent, military equipment is made by the same factories that produce goods for the civilian economy, and yet the military equipment is usually much better. The difference is quality control. When a factory is filling a military order, an officer is on the premises. If it is a big order, there may be a number of officers. They are empowered to reject any item if they think it is substandard, and the factory must either make it right or produce another one. I learned about this from an engineer with extensive experience in military industry. He had once been in a transistor factory, he told me, which was trying to fill a military order. The Army's inspector would accept only two or three of every 100 transistors the factory was making.
>
> The man who worked in the factory that makes electrical equipment for ships, described earlier, told me what happened when his enterprise had a contract from the Soviet Navy: 'The Navy people don't mess around. An ordinary customer is different. You can tell him, "Take it easy, we'll have it ready for you tomorrow," things like that. But the Navy man won't listen to that kind of talk. When he comes, everybody bows down to him and listens to him as though he were a god. What he says goes.'"[51]

Quality control, of course, is frequently rigorous throughout any arms economy. But how different is the underlying American economic process! Competition drives it forward, and as two prominent specialists tell us, this may "be so fierce that without expansion many companies would not be able to survive".[52] Cyclical crises accompanied by price movements, uneven development and utilisation of capacity, and inflation provoke mergers, rationalisation, transnational links and takeovers, and conglomerate product diversification. The multinational corporations which rocketed into life in the USA and Western Europe after the Second World War, drew life from, and ultimately caused the extinction of, the post-war Keynesian world order, by recruiting nation states in their support whilst undermining the power of those states to regulate their own economic and social policies. Starting from the USA, military producers quickly joined the transnational race, and helped push forward both the cold war arms race and half a hundred lesser military markets in hot spots all around the world.

Looked at from the vantage point of the USA, these companies found space to grow in the spare technological capacity of the vastly productive American economy. Thompson is right to stress how far the Military Industrial Complex monopolises Research and Development costs, especially Governmental R and D. More: it has also monopolised the third industrial revolution. President Reagan's fearful programme of "star wars" most surely has a very "rational" intention of assuring an American lead over Japan and Germany in these vital technologies. But even if it works, precisely *what* will exercise this lead? The state structure which promotes the leading process will remain lowly profiled, and it will be a range of giant transnational corporations which will continue their aggrandisement, develop their capacities and maximise their profits. The word "profit" may frequently be used with vulgar disregard for realities: but those who try to dispense with it will lose a key concept for the analysis of militarism, even if we have entered a new "exterminist" age.

Of course, there is a logic of military development, which shapes the pattern of investment and reward. As Marek Thee tells us:

> "The most crucial and sensitive link which internally impels the arms race is military R&D. This is the machinery and engine working incessantly on the improvement of old and the invention of new weapon systems. It is the goal-setting, the mode of operation and institutional set-up of military R&D which generates the technological momentum behind the arms race.
>
> The development of new weapon systems requires long gestation periods: 10 to 15 years are needed for the conceptualisation, prototype production, repeated testing and perfection of the new arms. This factor invests military R&D with constancy and permanency. Its operation tends to transcend ephemeral and volatile political processes in the external environment, including arms control and disarmament

negotiations. Its innovation rate tends to outpace these negotiations, relegating them to debates on obsolete weapons and making their outline largely irrelevant.

Reinforcing this "permanency trait" in the operations of military R&D is the routine to follow up automatically each innovation in defence with an effort to complement it with counter-devices in offence, and *vice versa,* in a constant spiral chain reaction of offence and defence. Perpetuity is thus inherent in the operation of military R&D. In the process, military R&D grows and expands. Its functioning is greatly actuated by inner impulses. Knowing less about the performance of the adversary and more about its own achievements, its expansion and growth propensity is fuelled largely by its own exploits. It ends up racing against its own achievements. A kind of square action-reaction-overreaction phenomenon comes into being, fed both by outer and inner impulsion.

The technological momentum produced by military R&D exerts a pervasive impact on the ways in which problems of peace and war are approached. New weapon systems serve as an inspiration for new political departures. The moment they enter the production line and become available, these start to figure high in the political-military game. They corrupt the political process. In the end, the whole architecture of international politics is affected by the race in military technology."[53]

Indeed, President Eisenhower could see this awesome development shaping up, and devoted his farewell address in 1961 to warning about it. His words may now be seen as prophetic.

"This conjunction of an immense military establishment and a large arms industry is new in the American experience. The total influence — economic, political, even spiritual — is felt in every city, every state house, every office of the Federal government. Yet we must not fail to comprehend its grave implications. Our toil, resources and livelihood are all involved; so is the very structure of our society.

In the councils of government, we must guard against the acquisition of unwarranted influence, whether sought or unsought, by the military-industrial complex. The potential for the disastrous rise of misplaced power exists and will persist.

We must never let the weight of this combination endanger our liberties or democratic processes. We should take nothing for granted. Only an alert and knowledgeable citizenry can compel the proper meshing of the huge industrial and military machinery of defence with our peaceful methods and goals, so that security and liberty may prosper together.

Akin to, and largely responsible for, the sweeping changes in our industrial-military posture has been the technological revolution during recent decades.

In this revolution, research has become central; it also becomes more formalised, complex, and costly. A steadily increasing share is conducted for, by, or at the direction of, the Federal government."

Lord Zuckerman has reminded us that Eisenhower himself suffered considerably at the hands of this very powerful complex. Kistiakowsky, who devised the implosion system for the earliest atom bombs, held the post of Chief Science Adviser during the Eisenhower years, and his biography revealed how the President's policies "were always frustrated by those who consistently exaggerated the Soviet military threat".[54] But it will be difficult to sustain Zuckerman's view that "It is . . . the technician . . . who is at the heart of the arms race."[55] Behind the technicians stand the corporations, and in the Western world, the corporations must expand or go bust.

Having said all this, we have not arrived at a point at which we can vindicate the rationality of capitalist militarism. It may be rationalism (if not necessarily of the highest order) not to allow oneself to go bust. But there is some evidence for the view that, contrary to the expectations of the participants, high arms spending may correlate with low productivity overall and sluggish innovation. The work of Seymour Melman is instructive on this count.

There is a further weakness in the view that the two superpowers "do not *have* but *are* military industrial complexes". It does not allow for degrees of relative autonomy of political processes. Is there *no* difference between, say, the administrations of Nixon and Reagan? On the lesser scale, among clients, are Thatcher and Macmillan the same thing? This view is not only over-simple, it is also over-pessimistic, because if rampant and unaccountable military formations had taken over their respective societies, the scope of oppositional forces would necessarily be sharply restricted. Thatcher, of course, also differs from her American mentor, in the small degree to which she is influenced by the needs of domestic industrial capital, which has hardly prospered at her hands. In Britain it seems that it is trans-national capital which has normally been calling the tune, to an even greater extent than elsewhere.

However, there could be no clearer demonstration of the autonomy of these state processes than the recent scandalous episode of the Falkland (Malvinas) war. Innumerable multinational interests were anxious to reach a settlement with Argentina which could painlessly transfer the Falkland Islands from British rule. A succession of meetings had proposed quite radical formulae by which this goal might be achieved. What pressure brought the British Foreign Office to seek such a change? There was no desire among the inhabitants of the Islands to change their allegiance. Indeed, after the Argentine occupation, there was bitter recrimination from the islanders about the way they felt their interests to have been neglected. No, it was that part of transnational industry which is interested in the development of off-shore resources, especially oil, which sought a suitable political environment in which to begin such development. The resignation of Lord Carrington from the British Cabinet, immediately after the Argentines landed on the Islands, showed little instinct for self-criticism: indeed, wiseacres at the time said that Carrington had sacked Thatcher, contrary to the official report on the matter. Mrs Thatcher's subsequent war defied the United Nations Resolution 502. It also exacerbated the political crisis for the United States throughout the Americas, and still renders difficult the management of major banking deficits at a moment when the world banking system is stretched almost beyond endurance. Further, of course, it is widely held to have won her the 1983 General Election in Britain. No-one can doubt Mrs Thatcher's fidelity to capitalism: although it might be difficult to find significant capitalists who would have advised her to behave as she did. Equally, no-one believes that she was pushed into war by her military-industrial complex. The main force involved, the Navy, was about to be seriously curtailed for economy reasons, and the flagship had been sold to Australia. Although the Admirals are likely not to be displeased by the official lessons drawn from this conflict, and although they have since replaced a quantity of old equipment, no-one can attribute any causal role to such a beleaguered force.

Whatever autonomy States maintain, however, the thrust to war cannot be denied, and if "barbarism" is an emotive word, imprecise in its meaning, it nonetheless evokes appropriate responses. "Exterminism", if it is simply a literary coinage, is no worse a word. But as an analysis of the causality of the arms race, it is deficient, and needs to bring its feet back to the earth on which Luxemburg stood, if it is to seek real answers. What is the relationship between economic crisis and war; slump and the arms race; monetarism, militarism and the multinational corporations? How do military formations fit into the real power structures which sustain and promote them?

E.P. Thompson has given a notable impulse to the new movement for non-alignment, and few will doubt the practical significance of this. Luxemburg would have given him high marks:

in the beginning was the deed. But the political theory of non-alignment still requires its exponents who will need to analyse not only the undoubtedly real phenomenon of hegemonism,[56] and, for instance, to explain conflicts between "socialist" states, but who will also seek to do far more than has yet been attempted to explore the relations between these matters and that desperate world crisis of capitalism in which all of us are now caught.

That is why it is wise to pay attention to Ernest Mandel, who certainly has the capacity to help throw light on such matters, and whose discipline is, in any event, more relevant to our needs than that of psychoanalysis, much though this might tell us about some of the great men who are so busily jeopardising all our futures.

VII: Can our Rulers Rule the Bomb?

(a) The mutation in weaponry

However, if Mandel is right to resist the notion that irrationalism is in command everywhere, and if he can offer Edward Thompson some important corrections to his thesis, Mandel himself is too over-optimistic in his radical Cartesianism. "The possessing classes", he tells us, possess, among other things, "the instinct for survival (in the physical sense of the term)". "These people", he tells us, "constitute the richest ruling class that the world has ever known. To imagine that they would be ready to sacrifice all this wealth, this luxury, at any moment or in any circumstances, on the altar of abstract ideas . . . is completely to misunderstand the motivations of the pattern of behaviour of this class". Unfortunately, the consciousness of these potent sybarites is not in control of all or perhaps any of the military nuclear processes, and most of them are not at all likely to share in any process of consultation about whether the time has come to sacrifice their privileges. Which precise members of these possessing classes will be asked about whether to enter Armageddon or not? How will the plebiscite be arranged, and how long will it take? As the arms race rushes forward, the timing of decisions becomes ever more critical. The nuclear face-off between Pershing II missiles in West Germany, and SS20s and 21s in East Germany and Czechoslovakia, brings the time between launch and impact down to a matter of minutes. Solid fuel missiles do not go through the lengthy and visible process of being readied for firing, which rendered a previous generation of weaponry liable to detailed warning scrutiny by spy satellites. This is a key fact underlying the most recent mutation in doctrines of nuclear war.

Responding to the imminent deployment of cruise missiles in Britain and elsewhere in Western Europe, the Novosti Press Agency circulated an article by Vladimir Bogachyov, under the slogan "Parity will be Preserved":

> "The US Pershings and cruise missiles" said Mr Bogachyov, "if they are deployed in Western Europe, will really increase the threat to the Soviet Union and its allies. But these US nuclear systems will in no measure strengthen the security of Western Europe. Quite the contrary, irreversible retaliatory measures of the Soviet Union, deployment of new missiles which will take 4-5 minutes to reach targets in the FRG and Britain will place European NATO countries in a position similar to the position of the USSR and other socialist countries.
>
> In that case leaders of European NATO countries will have to experience what it is like to wait for Washington's further military ventures of a 'limited', 'protracted' or 'demonstrative' nature while sitting on a powder keg they placed on their land themselves.
>
> Who will gain from such developments? Naturally, not the people of Western Europe.
>
> The decision of socialist countries to start preparation for the deployment of Soviet missile complexes of the operational-tactical designation of the territories of the GDR and the Czechoslovak Socialist Republic is an enforced measure, but the measure that is absolutely necessary for the ensurance of the security of the Soviet Union and its allies in the Warsaw Treaty. Socialist countries take this step only in answer to actions of the United States which is now concluding the preparation for the deployment of new medium-range missiles in Western Europe."[57]

Within the rules of the nuclear game, this was an entirely predictable response. But at the same time, Soviet spokesmen have repeatedly insisted that these very tight time schedules will impose upon them a policy of launch on warning. This will have the effect of removing the decision about whether to respond to a real or unreal attack from direct human agency. Since the Soviet computers which will soon replace human judgement lag far behind American ones, there are serious voices in America to be heard begging for the release of sufficient advanced computer technology to enable the Russians to get such a decision right. And this is not a joke: within a recent period of 18 months researchers counted no less than 147 false alarms on North American early warning systems.

European statesmen who have faced this threat, and it is a dire threat indeed, have registered their fears in the bluntest terms, in Washington itself. A notable example was set by Willy Brandt, at the Special Congressional Hearing of September 1983.[58]

(b) The advance of secrecy in national policy formation

Even when there is ample time for consultation, it does not necessarily take place. For instance, when the British Government decided to renew the ageing Polaris warheads, at a cost in excess of £1bn pounds, this decision was never reported to the British Cabinet, still less in Parliament, still less again within the councils of the then governing Labour Party. In fact, the decision was taken in a secret group of four senior ministers, who did not share the responsibility with any of their colleagues.[59] Thus, to tell us that "with some exceptions the bourgeois nation state *has* control over its weapon sector" is to offer a generalisation which can only whet the appetite. Which exceptions? How serious? Where? Within this opaque area, very serious misdeeds may be done, including acts which can lead to irreversible consequences.

(c) The displacement of power within the alliances

Even more problematic are the relations between states inside the great nuclear alliances. Here, the concept of superpower is not easily dispensable. The degree of military integration within the two alliances is obviously far advanced, whilst a plethora of diverging interests frays away at their real social and economic cohesion.

The interdependence of weapon systems inside the alliances equally clearly centralises the capacity to take initiatives, and restricts the scope for autonomous action by all the lesser members of such alliances to the most rudimentary levels. We can trace this process back to its formative days. During the Suez crisis of 1956, for instance, Soviet nuclear threats against the British and French Governments probably had small impact. What proved the decisive restraint on these two key members of the Western alliance was United States' disapproval. David Carlton, the biographer of Sir Anthony Eden, reports Eisenhower's displeasure, and his subsequent action, in the clearest possible terms. Ike summoned the American Ambassador to take actions which resulted in the displacement of Eden.

Here for instance, is Ike in conversation with Winthrop Aldrich at the London Embassy:

" 'Can you get together the two people you mentioned in your message, without embarrassment?' asks the President.

Aldrich: 'Yes, one of them I have just been playing bridge with. Perhaps I can stop him.'

President: 'I'd rather you talk to both together. You know who I mean? One has the same name as my predecessor at Columbia University Presidency (Butler), the other one was with me in the war (Macmillan).'

Aldrich: 'I know the one with you in the war. Oh yes, now I've got it.'

President: 'Could you get them informally and say of course we are interested and sympathetic, and as soon as things happen that we anticipate, we can "furnish a lot of fig leaves".'

Aldrich: 'I can certainly say that.'

President: 'Will that be enough to get the boys going?'

Aldrich: 'I think it will be.' "

Aldrich was right. The boys did get moving, and Eden was ditched.[60]

Somewhat wryly, Carlton contrasts the displacement of Eden with the elevation of Kadar in Hungary: a simultaneous event, in a symmetrical relationship on the other side.

That is what sometimes happens when the interests of lesser allies conflict with those of greater ones. The narrowness of more ordinary consultation between superpowers and their clients was clearly revealed in the 1973 Middle East crisis, as Sir James Cable of the British Foreign Office has pointed out. "At 11.41pm on the night of October 24 the United States Government, anxious to deter the Soviet Union sending troops to Egypt to intervene in the Arab-Israeli war, ordered all US military commands throughout the world to increase their readiness to Defcon III (I is war and II "attack imminent").

This alert naturally included the three US Air Force strike bases (with nuclear weapons) and the American Polaris submarine facility in the British Isles. At 1.03am on October 25 Dr Kissinger, then American Secretary of State, informed the British Ambassador in Washington of this unilateral decision."[61]

Sir James Cable joined the Foreign Office in 1947, became head of the Western Organisation Department in 1970, was subsequently head of Planning Staff until 1975, and a counsellor in the Contingency Studies Department. Not surprisingly he was a close student of Dr Henry Kissinger, and was able to perceive the significance of the Defcon III alert before this was spelt out in Kissinger's memoirs, which specifically discuss the repeated complaints by the subordinate allies about the lack of consultation in the critical episode, as Sir James now points out: "The allies were really objecting not so much to timing as to the absence of opportunity to affect our decision. But imminent danger did not brook an exchange of views and, to be frank, we could not have accepted a judgement different from our own . . . allies should be consulted whenever possible. But emergencies are sure to arise again; and it will not be in anyone's interest if the chief protector of free world security is hamstrung by bureaucratic procedure . . ." In fact, there was no "imminent danger". Sadat has told us that, far from straining to join issue, the Russians did everything they could to stop any Arab offensive, and actually delayed every consignment for six months during 1972-73 to enforce their views. This caution was a conscious application of detente politics, which were simultaneously applied by the Russians to the Vietnamese. It is rather difficult to believe that Kissinger, of all people, was unaware of this.

All this indicates that the rather nervous arguments about "dual key" control on nuclear missiles are distinctly theoretical. Paul Bracken, an American scholar who has produced the most comprehensive analysis of the organisation and management of nuclear command systems yet to become available, documents a number of similar cases. In 1980, the Americans concluded a defence pact with Turkey. It ran to 100 pages, but only six of these were ever submitted to the Turkish National Assembly. In Greece, again in 1980, the Greek Foreign Ministry refused to sanction the use of Greek bases for nuclear attack. "Despite this, the Greek Defence Ministry proceeded to sign an agreement with the United States anyway."[62]

(d) Control within the superpowers

But if subordinate "allies" have largely lost control of the decision about whether and about which issues they may or may not be taken to war, this does not mean that weapons deployed are in fact held under tight control even by the duly constituted authorities within the superpowers. Bracken shows that there exists a dangerous ambiguity in the command and control of nuclear weapons. The very existence of tactical nuclear weapons implies the de-centralisation of authority to fire. "On the other hand, for ICBM forces the system of alternative command posts and headquarters of various units makes it highly unlikely that firing authority would ever be given to individual launching crews." Licence to fire nuclear weapons, like any other pattern of military response cannot be effectively circumscribed without loss of efficiency which could be quite crucial. "An astronomical number of possible contingencies could arise from command structure breakdown." For this reason authority has to be delegated. Such delegation requires close scrutiny, but does not yet receive such scrutiny. Bracken finds the known details to be "necessarily sketchy". Nonetheless, he tells us: "the accounts of those close enough to be informed invariably point to presidential benign neglect". Even the "Football", the ceremonial orb of final destruction which is usually thought to offer the American President physical control of the decision to launch nuclear war, proves under this scrutiny to be a totemic object. Bracken cites a former Director of the White House Military Office who held office under every President from L.B. Johnson down to Jimmy Carter:

> "No new President in my time ever had more than one briefing on the contents of the Football, and that was before each one took office, when it was one briefing among dozens. Not one President, to my knowledge, and I know because it was in my care, ever got an update on the contents of the Football, although material in it is changed constantly. Not one President could open the Football — only the warrant officers, the military aides and the Director of the Military Office have the combination. If the guy with the Football had a heart attack or got shot on the way to the President, they'd have to blow the goddam thing open."[63]

In industry, when people speak of working to rule, they are referring to a total breakdown of established authority. When sufficiently rigidly enforced, rules stop anything from moving. There is no reason to suppose that military rules are intrinsically more benevolent. "Lines of authority are clear only in principle" says Bracken, "not in practice". Once again, Daniel Ellsberg offers a forbiddingly convincing example of the actual working of these tense processes:

> "Craziness is not the most immediate and serious problem. Misunderstanding and misguided judgement by one of the thousands of people is a much more serious possibility. For instance, during the study for CINPAC I questioned a particular major in Kunsan, Korea who had on his little airstrip, possibly closer to Communist territory than any other airstrip in the world, 10 F-100s, each of which had slung under it a 1-megaton bomb. This kind of weapon was not meant to be carried underslung; it had too high a risk of going off if it were dropped or if there was an accident. This man had under his command in that little strip 10 of those, the equivalent of five World War II's.

He told me what his orders were and if Jimmy Carter were to ask his counterpart today what his orders were, I'm sure he'd get the same answer — "I can't alert those planes, even for their safeguarding; I can't let them take off, let alone execute with direct order" (in those days from Osan, his higher base, or Kadena in Okinawa, or possibly Tokyo). The reason for those orders was that if he, on his own judgement, merely safeguarded his planes by having them take off (which other people did do more or less routinely), his weapons might go off. And if his weapons went off, all communications would go out in that area. The last thing that people would know was that in the course of an alert, either a false aarm or a real war, a thermonuclear explosion had just gone off on one of our bases. Their belief that the war was on and that they would get no further messages, including execute messages, would then follow.

So I asked the major, 'Quite aside from accidents, what would you do about your orders?' Since I had authority from Admiral Felt, he answered me: 'Despite my orders, I'm the commander of this base. It is the oldest principle of war that a commander has the right and authority to protect his troops. If I thought my troops were in danger, for example, if I heard of an accident, that is, an explosion, somewhere else in the Pacific during an alert, I would send them off.'

And I said, 'And what do you think they would do?'

He said, 'Well, you know what the orders are. They would go to a rendezvous area, reconnoitre, circle, until they got an execute order to carry out their plans, and if they did not get an execute order, they would return. Those are their orders.'

'And how would that work?' I asked.

'I think they'd come back. I think most of them would. Of course, if one of them broke out of that circle and headed for his target, I think the others would follow, and they might as well,' he added philosophically, 'because if they go, we might as well all go.'

Of course the major in Kunsan didn't claim *he* had been authorised to alert his planes; but he did refer to the President's delegation to Admiral Felt, which he clearly took as a precedent. At higher intermediate levels of command, like the Seventh Fleet, I was told by Atomic Control Officers that there existed secret delegations from CINPAC, paralleling the delegation to CINPAC by the President."[64]

Paul Bracken shows that the exigencies of command and control of nuclear forces defy tight and detailed executive decisions, even within the hegemonic state itself. Further, there is abundant evidence of recurrent pressure on the American Government itself to violate both domestic and international law in order to secure prompt military response to real or imagined threats.

We have seen the illegal bombardment of Cambodia, which was kept secret even from the secret files maintained by the Nixon administration, and which was a domestic scandal no less than a war crime according to the Nuremburg principles. Breaches of international law are more venerable than these domestic infractions, which nonetheless recur. President Johnson organised the invasion of the Dominican Republic in 1965, contrary to the Charters of the United Nations and the Organisation of American States, and contrary to the preamble and Article One of the North Atlantic Treaty itself. True, Johnson subsequently had recourse to the OAS for *ex post-facto* justification. More recently, United States' attempts to de-stabilise Nicaragua have included the deployment of large armies of mercenary soldiers funded by the Central Intelligence Agency in despite of both domestic and international law. The destruction of Nicaraguan oil terminals has been a further and more recent violation of the North Atlantic Treaty, the Charter of the United Nations, and the Charter of the OAS. The invasion of Grenada required similar breaches. The waging of war by illegal means obviously undermines the Constitution of the United States, and it is no accident that the Cambodian adventure and Watergate were coincidental in time. The breach of international law by the United States has provided a direct justification for the so-called Brezhnev doctrine, which was invented and invoked to cover the Warsaw Pact invasion of Czechoslovakia in 1968. Speaking in defence of this, Fidel Castro agreed that it was "illegal", but maintained that it was "necessary".

Because of divisions within the American polity, it remains difficult for American Governments to violate international law without arousing storms of political opposition at home. No doubt this welcome evidence of the humanity and democracy which remain so very alive, if so much held down in the USA, also constitutes a major pressure towards illegal and unconstitutional behaviour by officialdom. But when a President behaves unconstitutionally, it is difficult to argue that the social class which has mandated him retains any effective "control over its weapon sector". On the contrary, he deceives not only those of his countrymen who rightly oppose him in principle, but also all but the most intimate collaborators within his own circles of Government. This deceit is not the product of power, but of crisis.

In the course of this brief examination, necessarily confined to the American sphere of influence, we have seen that many decisions which are constitutionally the prerogatives of the separate nation states leagued into NATO have each been displaced, to become the monopoly of the dominant superpower, the United States. All these displacements signal areas of tension, potential conflict. If we are right to detect a consistent weakening in the relative economic strength of the United States, then it is a short step to predict that strategic monopoly must itself come under challenge, and sooner rather than later. In international relations, deceit of allies, or the overriding of their interests, not only removes their control of strategic decisions, but in the middle run will provoke a struggle to recover such control. This will in the future be difficult to withhold from economic equals. And it is precisely in this fracturing framework that a major peril could lie. Hegemony over a wide alliance gives the initiative, which will not readily be voluntarily put aside.

VIII: Balance of Power, Balance of Resistance

Mandel is right to reject the notion that the structures of the great nuclear powers are symmetrical, because their motors of economic effort are really different. However, he underestimates the degree to which entry into the nuclear game prescribes a certain symmetry of response.

President Andropov believes that

> "the appropriate balance of military forces including nuclear ones, between the states of the North Atlantic Alliance and the Warsaw Treaty states that is formed in Europe, objectively served the cause of European security and stability".[65]

Such "stability" presupposes a continuation of the division between Eastern and Western blocs, and if its maintenance depends upon maintaining a balance of military forces, then for each weapons development on one side there must be a matching response on the other. Needless to say, the development of a Soviet "deterrent" required no such "balance". Nikita Khrushchev once laconically pointed up this truth when he said that it was enough to be able to kill everyone in the United States once, and not necessary to be able to accomplish such a feat 50 times over. Andropov's response to the deployment of cruise and Pershing II missiles accepts no such deterrent outlook. Not only does it announce counter-deployment of appropriate intermediate range missiles in Czechoslovakia and the German Democratic Republic, which afford the possibility of response in a so-called "limited" exchange, and of a "first strike", even if these intentions are still denied: but also it insists that

> "corresponding Soviet systems will be deployed with due account . . . in

ocean areas and in seas. By their characteristics these systems of ours will be adequate to the threat which is being created to us and our allies by the American missiles that are being deployed in Europe''.

Within the rules of "balance" such a reaction was quite inevitable. But the same "balance" also implies the need for a worldwide ring of nuclear submarine bases, which ordinary citizens are liable to perceive as involving a degree of "expansionism". In a word, the rules of the nuclear game do impose their baneful logic on all participants, even if there will always be those who oppose this process in every power structure, capitalist or communist.

We have recorded above some of the details about Sakharov's resistance to the 57-megaton hydrogen bomb test undertaken at Khrushchev's insistence (see Chapter Six). It fully matches the more recent protests of Lords Mountbatten and Zuckerman, or the remarkable statements of George F. Kennan which have been published under the title *The Nuclear Delusion*.[66]

Opposition within the military and political elites will certainly recur. Nonetheless, we are bound to accept Mandel's dictum: "What is crucial for us . . . is an independent and democratic movement of mass mobilisation and mass action". Without such a movement, the prospect would be dismal. Those movements which have grown up in almost all Western and neutral countries in Europe, as well as that in the USA itself, have followed what Mandel calls a "unilateral" course. That is to say, they have sought to seize initiatives to change the policies of their own Governments, whether in respect of the deployment of particular weapons systems, or in respect of international alignments. A peace movement which does not address its demands to its own Government is in danger of becoming a platonic endeavour and its influence will then become academic. However, there are also international objectives which are as practical as national disarmament goals. For instance, the struggle to create agreed nuclear-free zones implies a convergence of national movements, with certain state interests, in which Romanians, Greeks, and Yugoslavs reach agreement with Bulgarians, or in which the Nordic countries arrive at their own collective solution.

The argument about the de-nuclearisation of central Europe does not imply a retreat into diplomatic pressures, but on the contrary, requires a major effort of political action and mass mobilisation.

The goal of a nuclear-free Europe offers other important national/international mobilising challenges. Other continents, as we reported above, also have aspirations to become nuclear-free zones. In Africa, the policy of the Organisation of African Unity has been to prohibit nuclear weapons from the entire continent, while in South America there is in force the first and only Treaty establishing a nuclear-free zone in a populated area. The enforcement of that Treaty, and the maintenance of the nuclear embargo in Africa both pose a challenge to the European peace movements which go beyond the imperatives laid down by Mandel, of "propaganda, protest, solidarity". These, Mandel tells us, are different from mass mobilisation and action for concrete goals. But solidarity action with those who are seeking to guarantee the non-nuclear status of other international zones may require very specific types of action.

Let us look at an agenda for such types of action.

The testing of a nuclear device in the South Atlantic was a direct challenge to the African nuclear-free zone. As South Africa moves towards acquiring the capacity to manufacture nuclear weapons, the front line states face a severe dilemma. I have discussed this above,[67] to show what happens when the arguments about nuclear deterrence so fashionable in the governing circles of NATO States are applied by other peoples, from other areas. This case puts it all in a nutshell: Mozambique, Angola and Zimbabwe suffer constant attack from South Africa already. Marauders destroy their military installations and dislocate their economies. A full-scale guerrilla war is maintained in Angola. International agreements about the trusteeship territory of Namibia are deliberately flouted. The Apartheid regime knows no binding laws to restrain its military policies. As the South African bomb goes into deployment, how can its intended victims respond? Do they not *need* their own nuclear deterrent? So far, their view has remained far more civilised than the prevailing myth which governs European chancelleries: they still seek their security and defence by forbidding all nuclear weapons in their region. Of course, if they were to be compelled to change their minds, then South Africa would have precipitated the nuclearisation of the entire continent, abruptly, just as a crystal dropped into a supersaturated solution can instantly rigidify its entire surroundings.

A Zimbabwe deterrent would not only answer South African provocations. It would also provoke an uncertain response in Zaire, the shock of which would judder northwards into the Arab world, as bomb answered bomb in a frightening process of deployment and counter-deployment, joining the natural response to Israeli nuclear weapons in the West Asian area. Obviously, the

OAU policy is more rational. But to implement it, and stay within its prohibitions, it will be necessary to prevent the South Africans from acquiring and installing nuclear weapons. Western Governments, which could do this, have not been at all willing to face up to their responsibilities. Western peace movements, however, once they had identified the multinational corporations which have been sustaining South Africa's nuclear programme, could boycott and blockade them in their home territories, whilst raising hell around the appropriate government departments in their own administrative centres. The development of transnational enterprise, and its intricate involvement in such villainies as these, renders vulnerable the whole destructive process, once it has become visible. The decisions of United Nations' bodies go far to legitimate such an opposition, without which the calls of the UN remain just but impotent. It is therefore much to be hoped that links may soon be established between the European peace movements and concerned people in Zimbabwe and the other front line states. Solidarity in this matter is by no means a matter simply of propaganda and abstract protest, but of very direct intervention against offending institutions, which are not South African, but British, French and German. It is also, as always, a matter of self-interest. There is no valid argument against nuclear proliferation from within official Western "deterrence" theory, which indeed positively incites new states to join the nuclear club. But those of us in Europe who oppose both Apartheid and its bomb will be able to share our influence for disarmament, if only we have given an effective measure of support to the Africans whose lives depend on restraining South Africa's developing capacity for war.

In the same way, public opinion in Europe can be invited to take responsibility for enforcing even the Treaty of Tlatelolco, which gingerly established the South American nuclear-free zone. There is considerable evidence that the British Fleet grossly violated this Treaty when it carried into the South Atlantic into the Treaty area a heavy arsenal of prohibited nuclear weapons.[68] Indeed, the flagship *Invincible,* has been forbidden to dock in Australia and Japan because of the poisonous cargo it carries. Obviously if a nuclear-free zone can be violated by the first nuclear power which gets into an argument, without any resultant action, then the whole United Nations' strategy for de-nuclearisation of major regions of the world has been aborted. But if strong and independent peace movements are determined to enforce such zones, they can reach out for, and apply powerful sanctions against those Governments which defy international agreements. In fact, in today's world, with the concentration of the physical power which we have been describing, diplomatic agreements alone will never suffice to restrain the drive to war. Only the most vigilant public opinion, backed by the capacity for popular action, can preserve the peace. A determined and organised people is the necessary response to the still growing menace of the nuclear bomb. Daunting though it may be, the agenda which this implies requires the building of a fully international network of contacts.

IX: People against Nuclear Proliferation

There are two kinds of nuclear proliferation racing ahead throughout today's world. 'Vertical'' proliferation, which has been the main preoccupation of this discussion, takes place in the runaway competition between the two major powers. ''Horizontal'' proliferation consists in the steady enlargement of the circle of states holding nuclear weapons. This second type of proliferation is all set to take on frightening new dimensions. The development and exportation of nuclear reactors diffuses the technical capacity to prepare atomic weapons,[69] at the same time that the credibility of the Non-proliferation Treaty has totally broken down. The nuclear powers were able to persuade smaller states to forego the advantages of ''deterrence'' because they promised to restrain, and then diminish the size of their own arsenals. At the beginning of this decade, their failure to do any such thing was duly noted in the first decennial review conference of Non-proliferation Treaty signatories. The superpower policemen were never admired in their nuclear role, but they were formerly capable of securing a minimal compliance. Now this capacity is clearly failing. Already, the Indian ''peaceful explosion'' has provided the incentive for similar bangs in Pakistan; Iran may not be far behind. Insistent chatter speaks of a Libyan bomb. All kinds of informed speculation point fingers at this or that Latin American state, Tlatelolco notwithstanding. The moral impasse in which the Non-proliferation Treaty has arrived is perfectly exemplified by the case of Pakistan. All appropriate sanctions were imposed on arms supplies to that country when irrefutable evidence of its preparation of nuclear weapons was discovered. Immediately after the Soviet invasion of Afghanistan, the United States resumed arms shipments on an intensified scale, thus revealing that strategic considerations overrule all moral obligations whatever, even those involving nuclear matters.

This kind of thing perhaps explains the urgent popularity within some of the nuclear-armed states of the idea of a nuclear freeze, but it does not necessarily justify such an idea to those other states which are feeling the weight of external imperial pressures. Neither will it necessarily prevent the extension of nuclear armaments to new imperial centres. As we argued in Chapter One, "deterrence" has always up to now been essentially a bi-polar game, and the complexities involved in changing its rules to accommodate 12 or 20 players are fearful in the extreme. If the security of nuclear-free zones cannot be enforced, then all states which desire their independence will be forced into a race to nuclearise their military forces. The demand for a freeze is evidently reasonable when it is presented within the main arena of the arms race itself, by the American peace movement. Between the superpowers, few could oppose so sensible a move. It will not, however, be seen as similarly reasonable in the front lines of the Third World, once nuclear threats have been made against them. To freeze an unacceptable *status quo* was never just, and now it is fast becoming impossible. The Non-proliferation Treaty was imposed by the nuclear powers. Those powers are quite incapable of enforcing a freeze while they are themselves the most desperate carriers of fuel to the nuclear furnace. All their homilies in international agencies will be endured by people who are understandably deaf. Western military-industrial formations, with the nuclear-power industry, are giving a massive push to "horizontal" proliferation. While Mandel insists upon the connection between capitalism and militarism, he has little to say about this terrifying threat. Surely it cannot be argued that Western Governments have been acting in a rational, still less a responsible way, when they have afforded openings to so many new states to develop their own nuclear weaponry?

If technical and geographical proliferation undermines the rational controls which Mandel imputes to Western ruling groups, it also offers graver perils than he has conceded. It follows that we cannot afford to neglect any potential ally in the resistance to those perils, whether official or unofficial, secular or religious, red or "green". And while the peace movements must develop as a coherent and radical force, determined to pull out nuclear militarism by its roots, they will also need to address themselves to existing international forums, such as the United Nations or the Non-aligned movement. In so doing, they may discover their particular proposals, say, for nuclear-free zones, or for the international control of nuclear energy, can receive support from otherwise reactionary Governments which either resist the logic of great power rivalry, or are for other reasons open to pressures from peace movements. Peace movements, for their part, will be heard in the Third World to the extent that they are able to replace nuclear deterrent power with the force of solidarity. It has been the burden of this argument that such solidarity can be stronger than the force of arms, even nuclear arms. Of course, a bomb is a bomb, while solidarity has many names. Even today, it is often labelled as "Christian love", or found hiding under a variety of other ethical prescriptions.

X: Socialists and the New Resistance

How do the new international imperatives relate to the organisations and traditions of the Labour movement? Do they render obsolete the old socialist watchwords as some have claimed? In my view, Mandel is quite right to criticise some peace activists for adopting what he calls "the stance of 'farewell to the proletariat'". Whatever changes are taking place in the social structures of the advanced countries, it remains very clear that without the support of working people, it will be quite impossible for peace movements to reach working majorities within those countries. Moreover, whatever the failings of traditional workers' parties, the Labour movements do still embody the secular traditions of internationalism and anti-militarism. Both the successes and the failures of this tradition have an urgent relevance to us today, furnishing an invaluable resource for those seeking to create new awareness of the perils under which we now live.

The peace movements have brought about a great upsurge of conscience and self-organisation, much of it from beyond the traditional scope of the workers' movement. In the Churches, among women, in 'Green' campaigns and elsewhere, powerful links have been shaped.

But the necessary breadth of the peace movement does not mean that it can avoid the fundamental questions raised by social crisis. As Raymond Williams very wisely pointed out in the debate on Thompson's paper on "Exterminism", the drive to war and the burdens of slump are intricately interconnected.

> "It is", he wrote, "fortunately, still possible to generate movements for peace and for disarmament on the most general human grounds. That these are again growing is a significant gain against the culture and politics of violence. Yet alike for their intellectual adequacy and for

extension of their support it is necessary to reach beyond the moving and honourable refusals on which many of them still characteristically depend. To build peace, now more than ever, it is necessary to build more than peace. To refuse nuclear weapons, we have to refuse more than nuclear weapons. Unless the refusals can be connected with such building, unless protest can be connected with and surpassed by significant practical construction, our strength will remain insufficient.''[70]

''Still'', because, of course, it has happened before, over and over: the Labour movement was the first modern peace movement, and its earliest attempts at international organisation were quite precisely aimed at facing the agenda which Raymond Williams reaffirms.

Modern peace movements seek to stop particular wars, especially the next one. But the Socialist movement has sought to find ways to remove the causes of war, and this not only remains a desirable goal, but it is obviously now an overriding necessity.

Given the conditions prevailing in today's world, the goals of the peace movement and the goals of socialism are interlinked. So long as it survives capitalism sows the seeds of war, and so long as militarism bestrides the globe the aspirations of socialism will be denied and falsified. It is one thing that we face several imperialisms. The fact that the international organisations of Labour are divided, is another. Yet another is that on various sides we see not one, but several, ''actually existing socialisms'', sometimes actually at war with one another. All this can only serve to heighten the need to resume responsibility for Raymond Williams' agenda. Clearly, it is not enough to repeat old prescriptions, since some of these have already been found to involve unwanted side effects. We have spoken already about the damaging confrontation between the USSR and China. Such a crisis is not unique either.

Several States with governments claiming allegiance to Marxism invaded Czechoslovakia in 1968, to depose a deviant communist leadership. Vietnam more recently invaded Kampuchea, and was thereupon itself invaded by China. In Poland today, a military junta headed by a General who became chief of his country's general staff on the eve of its invasion of Prague, is tragically embattled against a domestic trade union movement which retains vast, (and although we may not be sure, probably majority) support among Polish working people. Such crises will very likely recur until all these official Marxisms can diagnose their causes, and agree upon radical, democratic and non-dominatory responses to them. Such responses would of course remove other major impediments from the progress of socialism.

In the statutes of the First International, which specifically restricted its scope to Europe, it was laid down that its Central Council should ensure "that the questions of general interest mooted in one society be ventilated by all and that when immediate practical steps should be needed, as, for instance, in case of international quarrels, the action of the associated societies be simultaneous and uniform."

This presumption of the founders of that International was based upon a sentiment expressed by Marx, but reflecting two generations or more of working class experience:

> "In contrast to old society, with its economical miseries and political delirium, a new society is springing up whose international rule will be *Peace,* because its national ruler will be — everywhere the same — Labour!"

Wars between States governed by people styling themselves "socialists", we may therefore presume, would have given strong offence to those founding spirits upon whose legacy all the modern contenders are anxious to draw.

There is a first elementary lesson for socialists to draw from this. Detente, which is above all necessary in an age where humanity literally faces nuclear extinction, evidently needs first of all to apply itself between states calling themselves socialist. It is surely a crying outrage, a shame upon socialism, that communists in different countries should find themselves called upon to kill each other in pursuit of these national communist wars.

This may not be a very "theoretical" insight, but it is nonetheless fundamental. We are bound to remember that Lenin and his colleagues thought it right to split from the second international because it was incapable of preventing or resisting imperialist wars. What such people would have thought about *socialist* wars boggles the mind. But once they have broken out, socialist wars are all too like any other war. War is war. When the killing starts, everybody involved faces an imperative need for rationalisations which can explain it away. These involve a species of ideology, in the pejorative sense of the word, which needs to locate non-socialist elements in the conduct of the adversary. Such elements undoubtedly exist in every "socialist" country without exception, and it does not require elaborate analysis to pinpoint them. Internally, the press of every such country frequently identifies some of them, albeit often belatedly or imperfectly. But truthful explanation of the major event of war requires a somewhat wider perspective than is offered in such rationalisations. Relations which have become impossible must have sprung from defective foundations, and it is to those foundations that we would have to look, if we were to pass beyond propaganda justifications to more genuine insights. Obviously this would involve us in the need to understand the sociology of socialist states, but that is another discussion. The other critical question which must not be passed over remains: what can explain the all-to-obvious collapse of communist internationalism, over and above the assertion of narrow state interests?

Internationalism is not, of course, reducable to the institutions which seek to embody it. Those who split from the Second International after 1914 in the schism which so deeply preoccupied Rosa Luxemburg, with whose views we began this discussion, claimed that their break was justified by that very same internationalism, since the Stuttgart Resolution on militarism and international conflicts had become a dead letter for the predominant leaderships within the International organisation, with the outbreak of the First World War.

The Stuttgart Congress of 1907, had been the first such gathering ever to be held in Germany itself, and it was organised with great show and no small expense. Nonetheless, it was becoming a battleground in which the German hosts were implicitly indicted in spite of their sponsorship, and explicitly criticised for their embourgeoisement. The debate on the threat of war produced several options. One, that of a general strike against war, had been rejected at previous Congresses. Another, that of Guesde and most of the French delegates, was to await a socialist victory which would remove the causes of war, and therefore settle the problem. A third trend was expressed by the majority of the Germans, emphasising the need to abolish standing armies and committing socialists to use all means to stop war breaking out or to end it once outbreak had actually taken place.

Lenin and Rosa Luxemburg proposed that the outbreak of war, which would weaken the hold of the capitalist state machines, should be the basis for efforts to overthrow their rule. A drafting committee stitched together the opinions of these various very different tendencies. It included Bebel, Vollmar, Jaures, Guesde, Adler and Luxemburg. The Stuttgart Resolution which emerged from their deliberations began with a strong reaffirmation of German social democratic orthodoxy and concluded with two

paragraphs which were pure Lenin and Luxemburg. It is interesting
to detect the other influences which mark its different sections,
because it is clear that there was something in it for almost every
current present within the International. Accordingly, it was
carried by acclamation verging on rejoicing.

The collapse of this programme is in retrospect not altogether
surprising, and indeed, from their respective viewpoints, both
reformists and revolutionaries had anticipated just such an
outcome. The First World War exploded many very general
socialist assumptions. As an institution the Second International
had proved impotent, but internationalism remained a powerful
force for all that. Its ideals were, if anything, strengthened in the
crisis which discredited its institutions.

This separability had been specifically noted by Marx in his
Critique of the Gotha Programme. That Programme had spoken of
working class emancipation "first of all within the framework of
the present day national state, conscious that the necessary result of
its efforts, which are common to the workers of all civilised
countries, will be the international brotherhood of peoples". In the
opinion of Marx this degree of internationalism did not deserve
high marks. Gloweringly bestowing his delta minus, he dismissed it
with the comment that it stood "even infinitely below that of the
free trade party". As he pointed out, that bourgeois party "also
does something to make trade international and by no means
contents itself with the consciousness that all peoples are carrying
on trade at home". The sin of the Gotha Programme was that it did
not emphasise *"the international functions* of the German working
class". In the beginning was the deed!

We may indeed suspect that for certain minds the existence of
international institutions is an excuse for ignoring international
duties. The Marxian notion that the German working class had
"international functions" was quite independent of any
institutional forms. As Marx specifically insisted "The
international activity of the working classes does not in any way
depend on the existence of the International Working Men's
Association. This was only the first attempt to create a central
organ for that activity; an attempt which was a lasting success on
account of the impulse which it gave but which was no longer
realisable in its first historical form after the fall of the Paris
Commune."

There is an abundant experience, coming down to our own days,
of the keen and effective exercise of these "international

functions" outside any fixed institutional forms. Innumerable movements of solidarity, with Algeria, with South Africa, with Vietnam, with Latin America, or with the Portuguese colonial territories have aroused very general support in working class movements around the world, which support has weighed far heavier than any imaginable inputs by particular international agencies.

Nonetheless, the growth of the transnational range of capital has already for a long time been imposing certain functions on working class oppositions which can no longer be intelligently conducted without some minimal degree of convergence and co-operation. The present deep economic crisis has served to make this very plain, in its own right. But slump and unprecedented mass unemployment also join with militarist responses by governments to threaten all the achievements of the working class movements in the most advanced capitalist countries, and these threats are already taking serious effect on the institutions which were evolved to uphold welfare, social security and labour rights, even while war is still only an item on the future agenda. Economic crises, and war preparations, menace the major institution of democracy itself. Trade unions cannot operate adequately when 10, 15 or more per cent of the adult population is without work. The humane social advances which followed the Second World War in Europe have all been jeopardised, and most are directly attacked, by the policies of monetarism and retrenchment which accompany hysterical expansion in the field of war preparations.

At the most rudimentary level, there evidently has to be a coming together of socialist and radical groupings with the new peace movements if the arms race is to be resisted and reversed: and there has at the same time to be a movement towards closer co-operation between labour movements in the fields of economic policy, if these oppositions are to project any credible alternative to slump and de-industrialisation. At the European level, this work is already beginning, albeit on an *ad hoc* basis, and it raises questions to which we must return. At this point it is sufficient to mention this in order to underline the truth that whilst we do not "depend on the existence" of any particular structures to embody socialist internationalism, nonetheless, we must always seek to discover appropriate institutional connections to allow internationalist ideas and responses to develop a material bite.

A major part of the problem which the socialist movement confronts whenever it seeks to open this issue, is that the various models of international association are self-evidently inappropriate. No-one could seek to recreate any of the classic internationals with any rational expectation of success. As Heraclitus warned us, we cannot step into the same river twice. However, while polycentrism is much to be preferred to a false and oppressive monolith, there are great problems for attempts to think internationalism, if these become set in a mould of regional material interests.

Following the debacle of 1914, the approach of the Communist International was to establish a rigorous centralism. In the conditions which Lenin drafted for affiliation to the Communist International "the programme of every party that is affiliated to the Communist International must be endorsed by the ensuing Congress of the Communist International, or by its Executive Committee". Further, "all the decisions of the Congresses of the Communist International as well as the decisions of its Executive Committee, are binding upon all parties affiliated to the Communist International". These conditions established a model for a world party, but they did not at all establish the sociological conditions in which such a party could become effective.

The isolation of the Russian Revolution ensured that the Soviet Communist Party remained a preponderant influence in the new International, and this was soon codified after Lenin's death, in a famous polemic statement of Stalin's.

"There is one question which serves as a dividing line between all possible groups, trends and parties and as a test of whether they are revolutionary or anti-revolutionary. Today, that is the question of the defence of the USSR, of unqualified and unreserved defence of the USSR against attack by imperialism.

A *revolutionary* is one who is ready to protect, to defend the USSR without reservation, without qualification, openly and honestly, without secret military conferences; for the USSR is the first proletarian, revolutionary state in the world, a state which is building socialism. An *internationalist* is one who is ready to defend the USSR without reservation, without wavering, unconditionally; for the USSR is the base of the world revolutionary movement, and this revolutionary movement cannot be defended and promoted unless the USSR is defended. For whoever thinks of defending the world revolutionary movement apart from, or against, the USSR, goes against the revolution and must inevitably slide into the camp of the enemies of the revolution."

When the Comintern was dissolved during the Second World War, there is no evidence whatever that Stalin wished to repeal this guideline. But of course, the existence of a plurality of similar states meant that their defenders could with greater justice amend this statement by abolishing the words USSR wherever they occurred, and inserting the names of all the such states taken together. Indeed, if the expectations of the early socialists, including Marx, had been justified, we should either have been able to expect the adoption of a common polity by all of them, or failing that, to have inserted into Stalin's edict the separate names of any of these states, without fear that it could be rendered meaningless in so doing. Had this been true, it could have been written that an "internationalist would defend" Yugoslavia without reservation, or China without reservation, or Czechoslovakia without reservation. It is perfectly obvious that this kind of thinking is no longer taken seriously in any part of the Communist movement. Quite aside from whether one disapproves of particular policies of particular states, (which informed persons are quite likely to do!) the fact of war between them is the tragic *reductio ad absurdem* of this commitment.

And yet the proper recognition that there are now many different communist and socialist centres does not itself enable us to work out what should be the relations between them.

For all the advantages that their democratic structures afford them, it is the inability to solve this problem which has weakened the predominantly European influence of the parties of the Socialist International, in spite of the extremely interesting developments within each of the individual socialist parties during recent years. We reach a position in which we can see a variety of global regional contacts between socialist forces, which can easily criss-cross the boundaries of the old internationals, but which have remained caught within the bloc divisions which have been, until now, the pre-eminent fact of the post-war settlement. On a different plane, we can see many possibilities of extended links between socialists of different countries, world-wide, on particular issues. But this kind of process will normally be constrained by an inability to link one issue with another. There already exists a growing dialogue between non-aligned peace movements in most zones of the world. This may well become more structured over time. But it is not easy to see how such a dialogue could reach agreement on policies to reverse the trade imbalances between North and South, to end imperial domination, or to create alternative international economic institutions to contend with the power of transnational corporations.

It is in this context that the recent discussion in the Italian Communist Party takes on a significance far outside Italian frontiers. As Berlinguer reported in the Central Committee debate of January 1982 any new impulse towards socialism in the world depends upon a breakthrough in the most highly developed capitalist regions, "starting with Western Europe". This, however, requires a new internationalism, not only as a moral commitment, but as a functional response to the problems which European socialist parties have to face.

That is to say, neither of the present Governments in France and Greece will be able to overcome the effects of world crisis on their economies within the framework open to their purely national administrations. Increasingly, the co-ordination of national economic policies on an alternative international basis becomes an imperative before there can be successful attempts to solve national problems.

Already there are interesting meetings between socialists and some euro-communists, attempting to establish the necessary groundwork for the exploration of these issues. What has become known as the IPSE (Institute for Social and Political Economy) Forum has linked socialist economists and economic ministers, in developing an audacious project for European economic recovery. Surprisingly large numbers of those engaged in this work may also be found present in the discussions of the European Nuclear Disarmament Conventions, even though not all the national political parties involved in the convergence on economic policy have anything like the same wavelength on questions of disarmament. The trade unions involved in the END convergence have been working on a common programme for the conversion of military industries to civil production, which has brought major unions such as the British TGWU, the Italian metalworkers federations, the German I.G. Metall into close agreement. It is painfully clear that economic co-operation between European socialists becomes increasingly necessary if the foundations of European democracy are to be maintained. Slump and militarism are scorching the ground around us, and withering what yesterday were almost universal assumptions about the democratic bases of European politics.

XI: An Agenda for 2000

If we are to prevent the third world war, then, perhaps now it is necessary not only to demonstrate, but also to ask ourselves the question, where should we all be in the year 2000? All of us are conscious that it is not probable that humanity will survive so long. And yet, unless we can think through some rational responses to the problems which have exploded all these terrible local wars, unleashing all these millions of tons of conventional bombs on to the heads of peasant farmers, and starving all these millions of human babies, the very struggle for survival itself becomes less, not more effective. What is the prospect of a world beyond Atlanticism and the Warsaw Treaty?

Supposing that our Europe, from whose capital cities so many orders of battle have been issued, could begin instead to concert proposals for a joint response to the slump, as well as to disarmament, would this not lead directly to new political relationships? Over there is China, struggling in a giant plan to bring its billion people out of poverty by the same year 2000. Are not their needs and ours reciprocal? Could we not combine to plan our way out of the indefensible world which has emerged, where on one side vast productive forces rot, and on the other, people teeter daily on the edge of privation? With Europe meeting China, would not recovery and development increase demand elsewhere? What might then become of prospects for the planning of triangular trade to help development throughout the South? As oil prices rose again, would not the oil countries be encouraged to join their forces in this process? The momentum of such initiatives could surely, could it not, involve the Soviet Union in active co-operation? The American economy itself might, might it not, revive, (and psychosis decline?) as recovery took its course? Seeds of these utopian prospects are already sprouting. In their participation in the peace movement, socialists around the world are already marking out one experimental model in human co-operation, on the most urgent issue of all. But if, as they link their other initiatives, they can begin to extend these first, tentative and halting contacts into a continuing discussion, can they not thereby prepare the ground for a new world polity?

The fragmentation of the socialist bloc has up to now in many ways run far in front of the growing disaggregation of the North Atlantic Treaty. It will not easily re-fuse. In today's world there still remain two uneasy and fractured Alliances. Tomorrow's world will have to be *one,* which will either be a human community of United Nations, or a radioactive desert. If there is to be a road to world unity, it lies through self-determination of the peoples, and the development of a framework in which self-management of their institutions begins to be the means by which they learn to join human needs to social resources.

What kinds of institutions might promote and allow this new sense of common human destiny? To begin with, there is the United Nations. During these recent years, this organisation has begun to evolve quite radically, as non-aligned countries have increasingly forcibly tried to escape the logic of great power conflict, and to challenge the domination of one people by another. The advancing sweep of decolonisation and revolution has transformed the composition of the United Nations. Given this changing relationship of forces, there is no reason why the UN must repeat the futile trajectory of the old League of Nations. We would be blind if we did not see the enormous importance of the 1978 Special Session on Disarmament, simply because certain powers joined their forces to nullify the session of 1982. Similarly, the various responses to colonialism during recent years have expressed something of a worldwide movement of opinion, however much some imperial centres have obstructed or prevaricated. Of course the framework of the United Nations is grossly defective, but it is no longer possible to describe it as irrelevant. The permanent Security Council States can too often frustrate the majority in the General Assembly. Peace movements and radical political forces are already seeing the need to react to these kinds of decisions by the United Nations, especially where its agreements are being frustrated by great power initiatives. These movements are already convinced that this must be done, not merely by joining diplomatic lobbies, but where necessary, by opening major public campaigns. Next, we must all learn how to run in front, how to impose our own questions on the statesmen's agendas.

Only in this way can we overcome the weaknesses of populism, echoes of which are to be heard in the otherwise cogent appeals of E.P. Thompson to "the grassroots" and Ernest Mandel to "the workers' movement". It is agreed that the mobilisation (and self-mobilisation) of these groupings is a pre-condition for the shaping of public opinion, which has to become very strong indeed before we can win this argument. But there is no way that either peace or labour movements, separately or even together, can win the changes which we need outside those political processes within which they live and fear their deaths.

There is a terrible alienation to be overcome, and it can be stated very simply. People cannot disarm. States can.

The dominance of great nuclear powers over lesser allies, however, means that each alliance suffers innumerable shifts and strains, some of which run parallel to the needs of disengagement from the drive to war, and some of which confront those needs. At few times are nations able to act for disarmament simply in following the logic of their own policies. But for how long can they immunise themselves from the influences of an intransigent public opinion? And how much public opinion is needed to change the relationship of forces inside a state? The problem of disarmament has always been how to mesh together all those political forces which can bring help to any states which are trying to reject the pressures of the arms race, and weigh adversely against those which are not. An international campaign seeking to do this may find that governmental schizophrenia can even afford it space in which to grow. Conflicts of interest which might otherwise simply exacerbate dangers might thus assist the growth of peace movements.

The development of contact between the peace movements and their allies can help create the kind of United Peoples' movement which can begin to offer its own rewards to states which move to peace and non-alignment, and its own penalties to those which do not. Already there are continuing associations of peace movements in the Pacific zone as well as in Europe. It is entirely feasible to bring about much closer understanding between these different continental conferences. Means must also be found to encourage independent and non-aligned groupings in other global zones which have not yet established their own international fora to make their voices heard, and to join with all the others. But surely also, the socialist and radical parties, and the communist parties, must now begin again to talk to one another, if only to explore how difficult this is? If we all find it so impossible to see ourselves as part of common humanity, perhaps each should be invited to explain to the other how she or he thinks the world might be stitched back together before this century ends? Or before the world ends, which might all-too-easily be 10 years sooner?

Footnotes
1. *The Communist Manifesto,* Centenary edition, Lawrence and Wishart, 1948, pp.13-14.
2. *The Junius Pamphlet,* The Crisis in the German Social Democracy, Merlin Press, London, 1967.
3. Cf. Major General J.F.C. Fuller: *The Conduct of War,* Eyre and Spottiswoode, 1962, Chapter 8.
4. Luxemburg: *op. cit.,* p.9.

5. A.J.P. Taylor: *The Second World War,* Penguin 1976, p.229.
6. *The United States Strategic Bombing Survey, Overall Report (European War),* 1945, pp.72, 97.
7. I.F. Stone, The Hidden History of the Korean War, *Monthly Review Press,* New York, 1969, p.312.
8. Gabriel Kolko, War Crimes and the Nature of the Vietnam War, *Journal of Contemporary Asia,* Volume 1, No.1, Autumn 1970, p.6.
9. Arthur H. Westing and E.W. Pfeiffer, The Cratering of Indo-China in *Arms Control,* readings from the Scientific American, W.H. Freeman and Company, San Francisco, 1973, p.329.
10. William Shawcross: *Sideshow — Kissinger, Nixon and the Destruction of Cambodia,* Andre Deutsch, 1979, pp.298-9.
11. Ernest Mandel: The Threat of Nuclear War and the Struggle for Socialism: *New Left Review,* No.141, September-October 1983, p.24.
12. In *Europe versus America,* New Left Books, 1970, or in his polemic with Martin Nicolaus (NLR 59), Mandel's was one of the most determined socialist voices to insist that not one, but several, centres of capitalist power were in contention.
13. Frans A.M. Alting von Geusau: The Future of American-European Relations in *Allies in a Turbulent World,* Lexington Books, 1982, pp.156-162.
14. But not every national liberation struggle consistently strikes against the principle of imperial domination. Many seek to offset one capitalist power complex against another. Some succeed.
15. *Op. cit.,* p.25.
16. See *The Dynamics of European Nuclear Disarmament,* Spokesman 1981, p.212 *et sq.*
17. Mandel, *op. cit.,* p.26.
18. L.D. Trotsky: *The History of the Russian Revolution,* Vol.I, pp.56-7, Gollancz, 1932.
19. The Earl Mountbatten of Burma: The Final Abyss?, *Apocalypse Now?* Spokesman, 1980, p.13.
20. *Ibid.,* pp.9-10.
21. A large volume of smoke has been generated to screen the real implications of this argument from the public view. Nowadays the deployment of NATO intermediate range missiles is universally justified by reference to the SS20 missiles which have been deployed in the Western regions of the Soviet Union since 1978. Fifty of these missiles were in place during that first year of deployment, and more than 240 have been installed at the time of writing. However, NATO planning was not based upon the need to counter Soviet weaponry but upon the need to complete the possibility of graduated response. This was made perfectly clear in public NATO communiques during the earliest days after the December 1979 "two track" decision. We were reminded of the realities of this process when the *Observer* published excerpts from a collection of classified American documents, on Sunday 17 October 1983. Concerning Britain, these documents show

"that long before the Election of May 1979, the Labour Government had concluded that new missiles were inevitable. This would appear to make Labour's current opposition to cruise hard to sustain.

A secret State Department document written in February 1979, asserts that Mr Callaghan would not agree to anything before the election, and the Americans complained that his reluctance was 'complicating attempts for an early NATO accord'.

The papers go further; according to a briefing page, written in the autumn of 1978, Britain was prepared to use the NATO decision on new missiles to conceal its own plans to modernise its own seaborne nuclear missile force. Britain 'clearly perceives', say the document, 'that a NATO modernisation decision could be a political shelter for the nuclear decisions it must make by the mid-1980s'.

The documents go on to state that Mr Callaghan himself was convinced early on about the need to modernise, but was reluctant to support the arms control part of the 'dual-track' policy. The British, according to the documents, never believed in the efficiency of a separate European arms control agreement, and agreed to the arms control track only to accommodate the Germans and 'placate' left-wing elements in the Labour Party."

22. Mandel, *op. cit.,* p.28.
23. *Ibid.,* p.27.
24. Milton Leitenberg: Threats of the use of Nuclear Weapons since World War II — An Introductory Note, in *Problems of Contemporary Militarism*, edited by A. Eide and M. Thee, Croom Helm, 1980, pp.338 *et seq.*
25. "In the Spring of 1956, when we were in London and had talks with Messrs. Eden, Lloyd, Macmillan, Butler and other British statesmen, we told them frankly that we had rockets of various ranges. Later, when Israel, Britain and France attacked Egypt the Soviet Government stated in a message to the British Prime Minister: what would be the position of Britain herself if she were attacked by stronger states possessing modern destructive weapons of all kinds? And such countries, the message said, could even do this without sending a navy or an air fleet to British shores but could use other means, for instance rocketry. This statement by the Soviet Government evidently influenced them". *Khrushchev Remembers*, Andre Deutsch, 1971, p.435.
26. B.M. Blechman and S.S. Kaplan, *Force without War: US Armed Forces as a Political Instrument*, Brookings Institution, Washington DC, 1978.
27. Leitenberg, *op. cit.,* p.395.
28. Daniel Ellsberg, Call to Mutiny in *ENDpapers 1*, Winter 1981-82, pp.5 *et seq.*, Spokesman.
29. D.W. Eisenhower, *Mandate for Change*, Volume 1, Doubleday NY, 1963, pp.178-81. Ellsberg also cites Sherman Adams, Eisenhower's Chief of Staff at the White House:

"Long afterward, talking one day with Eisenhower about the events that led up finally to the truce in Korea, I asked him what it was that brought the Communists into line. 'Danger of an atomic war', he said without hesitation. 'We told them we could not hold a limited war any longer if the Communists welched on a treaty of truce. They didn't want a full-scale war or an atomic attack. That kept them under some control'."

In the above passage of his memoirs, Eisenhower also mentions: "Meanwhile, General Mark Clark (who had succeeded Ridgway as United Nations commander) began to suspect that the Communists were building up forces in the Kaesong 'sanctuary' area. He requested permission to launch an attack in the event he became convinced that a Communist attack there was pending. This authority I thought unwise to delegate at that time" (p.181). But recently declassified minutes of the National Security Council meeting on 11 February 1953, to which this refers, record a noteworthy exchange at this point, omitted from the memoirs: "(The President) then expressed the view that we should consider the use of tactical atomic weapons on the Kaesong area (an area of approximately 28 square miles, which was, according to Clark, 'now chock full of troops and material'), which provided a good target for this type of weapon. In any case, the President added, we could not go on the way we were indefinitely.

"General Bradley thought it desirable to begin talking with our allies regarding an end of the sanctuary, but thought it unwise to broach the subject yet of possible use of atomic weapons.

"Secretary Dulles discussed the moral problem and the inhibitions on the use of the A-bomb, and Soviet success to date in setting atomic weapons apart from all other weapons as being in a special category. It was his opinion that we should try to break down this false distinction.

"The President added that we should certainly start on diplomatic negotiations with our allies. To him, it seemed that our self-respect and theirs was involved, and if they objected to the use of atomic weapons we might well ask them to supply three or more divisions needed to drive the Communists back, in lieu of use of atomic weapons. In conclusion, however, the President ruled against any discussion with our allies of military plans or weapons of attack."

The corresponding discussion in Eisenhower's memoirs does raise the subject of allied attitudes (and perhaps, implicitly, those of the American public as well) in remarks that seem highly pertinent to a number of the essays that follow:

"If we decided upon a major, new type of offensive, the present policies would have to be changed and the new ones agreed to by our allies. Foremost would be the proposed use of atomic weapons. In this respect American views have always differed somewhat from those of some of our allies. For the British, for example, the use of atomic weapons in war at that time would have been a decision of the gravest kind." Cf. *ENDpapers 1*, pp.20-21.

30. Edgar Snow, *Red China Today, the Other Side of the River,* Penguin Books 1970, Chapter 76, pp.597 *et seq.*
31. Franz Schurmann, *The Logic of World Power,* Pantheon, NY, 1974.
32. Harry S. Truman, *Years of Trial and Hope,* pp.396 *et seq.*
33. Cf. Ken Coates, *The Crisis of British Socialism,* Spokesman, 1971, p.124.
34. Henry A. Kissinger, *Nuclear Weapons and Foreign Policy,* W.W. Norton Company Inc., NY 1969, pp.114-129.
35. Cf. Neville Maxwell: *Pacific Community,* Volume 1, No.4, July 1970, pp.561 *et seq.* Also cf. the summary by the same author in *The Times,* 13 June 1974.

Richard Hughes, writing in the *Sunday Times* on 16 April 1974, said, "Any possibility of a Moscow nuclear pre-emptive strike, which was seriously considered in 1969" could now be discounted "because China has since dispersed nuclear sites and could now immediately launch a counter-strike against Moscow and Leningrad from deeply entrenched missile sites along the Sinkiang border." Mr Hughes' estimate of the Chinese capacity for response seems, on the surface, to be a little excessive.

36. Enver Hoxha: Reflections on China, *Extracts from the Political Diary 1962-72,* Tirana 1979, p.439.
37. *ibid.,* p.440.
38. *Ibid.,* pp.447 *et seq.*
39. For an account of these extensive civil defence works, see *China Reconstructs,* April 1983.
40. David Holloway, *The Soviet Union and the Arms Race,* Yale University Press, 1983, p.87.
41. *Exterminism and Cold War,* Verso 1982, pp.1-34.
42. Marcuse: *Eros and Civilisation,* Routledge and Keagan Paul, p.4.
43. E.P. Thompson: Notes on Exterminism, the Last Stage of Civilisation. In *Exterminism and Cold War,* Verso, 1982, pp.4-5.

Later Thompson insists that he is *not* claiming that exterminism is a new and distinctive mode of production in the Marxian sense.

44. *Ibid.,* p.3.
45. *Which Way to Peace?* Michael Joseph, 1936, p.16.
46. R.L. Sivard: *World Military and Social Expenditures, 1982,* Washington, p.22.

47. SIPRI, *The Arms Race and Arms Control, 1983,* London, pp.155-167.
48. Thompson: *op cit.,* p.22.
49. I have extended this argument in my foreword to Alva Myrdal, *The Dynamics of European Nuclear Disarmament,* Spokesman, 1981.
50. The USSR and the Arms Race in *Exterminism and Cold War, op.cit,* pp.153 *et seq.*
51. Robert Kaiser, *Russia, the People and the Power,* Penguin Books, 1977, pp.323-4.
52. Tuomi and Vayrynen: *Transnational Corporations, Armaments and Development,* Gower, 1982, pp.2-3.
53. Marek Thee, *PRIO Report,* 3, 1982.
54. *Apocalypse Now?* Spokesman 1980, p.25.
55. *Ibid.*
56. This is the main weakness in the otherwise admirable text of the Medvedev brothers on Soviet involvement in the arms race.
57. Novosti Press Agency, 25 October 1983.
58. See *ENDpapers 6,* pp.97-102.
59. In this, the Wilson and Callaghan administrations were following a precedent established much earlier. Churchill had not informed Attlee, or any other Labour member of the wartime coalition, of the "Tube Alloys" project out of which emerged the Hiroshima bomb. When he took office, Attlee set up an *ad hoc* cabinet committee of "not more than half-a-dozen at most" of his most intimate colleagues, known nowadays from its file as 'General 75', to deal with the initiation of the British bomb. "Expenditure on atomic research and development was concealed under other heads. Interest by Parliament or the Press was not encouraged and Emrys Hughes, one of the few Labour MPs who tried to find out what was happening, complained: 'when we ask a question about it, one would almost think an A-bomb has been dropped' ". (Alan Bullock — *Ernest Bevin, Vol.III,* Heinemann 1983, p.185). But not only were cabinet ministers kept in the dark, and Parliament misled about the financial vote that was necessary. Even the secret committee was by-passed by a technical committee under the chairmanship of Sir John Anderson, a leading member of the opposition. By the time efforts were made to integrate the decision making processes, all the key decisions had already been taken. So much for parliamentary control, and so much even for cabinet government!
60. David Carlton: *Anthony Eden, a Biography,* Allen Lane, 1981, pp.460-1.
61. Sir James Cable, letter to *The Times,* 3 November 1983.
62. Paul Bracken: *The Command and Control of Nuclear Forces,* Yale University Press, 1983, p.171.
63. Gulley, *Breaking Cover,* p.213-2, cited in Paul Bracken, *op. cit.,* p.226.
64. Cited by Bracken, *Ibid.,* pp.228-9.
65. Andropov's Statement, 24 November 1983, Novosti.
66. Pantheon Books, New York, 1982.
67. Foreword to Alva Myrdal: *The Dynamics of European Nuclear Disarmament.*
68. Exchange of letters with United Nations (see Appendix).
69. Cf. Lewis A. Dunn: *Controlling the Bomb,* Yale, 1982: "Virtually all of the countries that might 'go nuclear' in the years ahead — Iraq, Pakistan, South Africa, South Korea and Taiwan, to name a few — already have the necessary theoretical knowledge." (p.24)

    "A somewhat controversial 1977 study by the Oak Ridge National Laboratory concluded that a country with only a moderate technological base — defined as including commercial distilling, oil refining, and other chemical processing industries from which parts could be taken: a basic machine shop and metallurgical competence; and light construction equipment — could clandestinely build a 'quick and dirty' spent fuel reprocessing plant in four to six months." (p.26).

Cf. also, George Quester: *The Politics of Nuclear Proliferation,* John Hopkins University Press, 1973, who registered earlier than many the basic inadequacy of the non-proliferation Treaty which "demands that all but five of the nations of the world renounce nuclear weapons; the authors of the Treaty naturally are among the privileged five. Some invidious response from other states is thus hardly surprising . . ." (p.233).

70. Raymond Williams in *Exterminism and Cold War,* p.85.

CHAPTER 10

Two Speeches
(i) Thou Shalt not Follow a Multitude to Do Evil

The closing speech at the Brussels Convention for European Nuclear Disarmament, July 1982.

This is a conference which you have all made. It is true that the aim we have been pursuing together involves us in efforts which are difficult and even contradictory. We have been trying to establish a form of association in which people can speak as directly as possible, one to another, across all frontiers of states and organisations, and in which they can exchange their ideas so as to be able to act more wisely.

At the same time we have been trying to avoid centralisation, hierarchy and bureaucracy. Therefore, of course, we have hit a considerable number of problems. There has already been reference to some of these, and I have collected a sheaf of additional comments on others. I think that all this experience must be discussed, and that it is necessary to learn from such a discussion in the continuation of our good work. It is pointless to talk to each other only about our successes and to rely only on them, because they will not repeat themselves if we do not understand our mistakes. We are aware of some successes, but we are also aware of many problems, and even of some failures. We must talk about those because that is the only way we can learn to avoid becoming like those people and those institutional forces which we abominate.

So I want to say something a little later about what I think are properly to be called our small failures, those which have inconvenienced some of you at these meetings, and those which can easily be avoided if we think fairly carefully together about what we want to do next.

But I must begin by talking to you about some great failures: because in this year there really have been some big ones. I

◀ *END Convention emblem.*

celebrate with Fenner Brockway and with our Japanese friend, the Venerable Sato, the enormous victory we shared when a million people affirmed their identity with us in New York. More, all of us celebrate the more than a million who have now twice consecutively appeared on the different streets of the major capitals of Europe. We all know about that, and we don't forget it. It is part of the culture which made this kind of meeting possible. It is that culture which makes us strong enough to face up to our failures.

Lucio Lombardo Radice has just very movingly turned our attention to one of these, in the Lebanon. We need a peace movement strong enough to forbid this kind of horror. I want to speak briefly about a second horror which we saw in the Falkland Islands. And I need to speak about this for two reasons. First, it is obvious that the Falkland Islands presented a crisis out of which the British people have not so far emerged with any credit or distinction whatever. I am frankly ashamed of that episode because I am a normally patriotic citizen of my own country. But we ought to say something else as well. There are lessons in our failure for all of you in Europe. Do you think that the cancer of rabid nationalism and chauvinism is incapable of infecting you? You too must study our failures. If you don't, you may repeat them.

In studying them there is one comment I have to make about an assumption which has permeated an important part of this conference, a part in which I have always made myself at home, among the rank and file peace activists. The assumption in question is one you have heard so many times, which expresses itself in the charge that we have, sitting here on the one hand, the peace activists; and on the other hand, the politicians.

Before I address this question directly I would ask you to bear with me in a short reminiscence because although I am actually a peace activist, I am also a permanent failure as a politician. And my most spectacular failure was several years ago, in fact about 16 or 17 years ago, when I was President of the Labour Party in Nottingham. We were very provincial and parochial, and our main concern was to try to secure the demolition of the largest tract or slum housing in Europe. We were passionately engaged in this project. But there was a war in Vietnam, to which all of us were strongly opposed. I was sent to the Labour Party Conference and given the mandate that we must oppose it. That was an instruction I could easily accept and so I spoke in the debate and criticised the Party leaders. They thought perhaps I criticised them too much because they expelled me from the Party.

As a result of my speech Bertrand Russell invited me to join the Russell Foundation. And I said to him, "well, you know I am not much use to you, because I have lost my platform. I am expelled. I am a man without an army, what can I do for you?" And he told me a story. He said, when he was a boy he was an orphan. He lived with his grandmother. At a very tender age she gave him a bible. In the bible she wrote on the flyleaf an inscription. The inscription said, "Thou shalt not follow a multitude to do evil". And it was on the basis of that political programme that I was very happy to join in with the work that Russell was doing.

Russell was also a failed politician. He tore up his Labour Party card in a rage at the complicity of the Party in the Vietnam war. But Vietnam is a matter of history and now we have seen what happened in the Falkland Islands.

What actually happened in this Falkland war? We had two completely barren islands composed largely of peat bogs, inhabited mainly by sheep, in a completely abandoned wilderness. For very many years, amounting to decades, we had totally neglected the interests of the people who are compelled to live there. They lived under the depredations of greedy companies which abandoned almost every attempt to enable them to live reasonably. At the time the Argentinians invaded, it was rather generally assumed that the British Foreign Office had been trying to find a way to cede these islands in order to be rid of them. But immediately after that invasion the British Task Force was sent southwards and the Falkland war broke out.

I apologise for taking your time on this war, because everybody knows, (have we not read it in the press?) that this was a small war. It was a small war. But I was thinking, you know, about this small war. Killed in it were approximately the same number of people who are sitting in this hall. In this small war, you three blocks, if it were possible to muster you from the dead souls, would be Argentinians. You two blocks would have drowned in the freezing water of the South Atlantic because the *Belgrano* was torpedoed. Over on that side are the dead souls from Britain. The Argentinian souls were young boys of 17 and 18 years old who had been conscripted. The English dead souls, we are told were volunteers. That means they were unemployed youth. We have three million people unemployed in Britain. Among young people unemployment is now a nearly universal expectation. Now friends, if you will imagine yourselves to be at my conference of dead souls, what do you say to this war?

"Thou shalt not follow a multitude to do evil."

The failure that we must face now is that when you look at this little war, which has killed a hall-full of people, where was our peace movement? You can't solve this problem by making a neat division between politicians and activists. I was involved, in the early days of the war, telephoning, frantically trying to find those who wished to protest against the despatch of the Task Force which created all this carnage. And I can tell you there were certainly many politicians who refused to be involved in this protest. I can also tell you there was an equally large number of peace activists who refused to be involved in it.

There is no simple explanation for this. When the first demonstration was brought together in London to express disagreement with this Falkland war it was led by some politicians who have been present at this conference. There at the front were Judith Hart, who spoke from this rostrum, and Tony Benn who spoke with Rudolf Bahro and Sergio Segre in the meeting place in the old market centre. Actively involved in the campaign was Stuart Holland, who is presiding here now. For their pains all these good people had their pictures printed in the daily newspapers in huge front page displays. They were ranged like criminals under the banner headline 'These are the enemies of Britain'.

At that time it was difficult to march for peace. At that time, not a quarter of a million, but 1,500 people walked through London, 1,500 people, all of whom were truly peace activists, led by these politicians. And I earnestly entreat our friends, all our friends, who are proposing this dichotomy between peace sheep and political goats to think about this problem. We must all think about it. I do not raise it as a reproach to the peace movement. Not at all: I raise it as a problem that we must understand, as a question we must discuss, as an item for our Berlin agenda. When people tell you we must stop talking and start acting, I say to them, yes we must have action. We certainly must have action. But this talk is absolutely necessary if we are to understand one another, and to learn from experience.

The Argentine boys who drowned and the British boys who caught fire like torches, burned like magnesium flares when they were hit by the Exocet rocket. They are not really here. They are dead. Now the war is finished, and everybody is in favour of peace in the Falkland Islands or the Malvinas. And we can now resume the agenda. But we have seen the failure of the peace movement in my country. We could not only not stop the killing: we had hardly begun the work of opposition to it before it ended. We have seen how, when this kind of crisis arises, volcanic social pressures are unleashed by our inability to find solutions to our economic incapacities, to our political blindness, and to the deep-structured drives that make militarism a more and more naturally accepted part of our cultures.

Yet out of this dire experience there are also positive lessons. Among the peace movement activists, to whom I spoke, there were some who were at first very reluctant to see that we should oppose the sending of the Task Force, that the war in the Falklands should be stopped before it could be started. Nonetheless within two or three days I found that the same people had become passionately convinced that this was so. Why? As often as not because they were on the telephone to some of you, because they were talking with some of you. And this is the other lesson we must learn. It teaches us about political communication. Outside of Great Britain you were not kept in that box where the media are controlled by seven transnational companies all telling the same tendentious story. Outside the box the reactions of Belgians and Italians or Greeks and Germans to the Falkland conflict were completely different from those inside. And so the communication which took place was really powerful as an antidote to the poison which had been injected into the British peace movement during this crucial moment.

Well, those are some thoughts about big failures. Now I must speak about how we are to collect the lessons of the small failures. We agree with some of the points made in debate about the earliest of our plenary sessions, and you understand our difficulty. A lot of people had to speak in order to show the vast range of support for European Nuclear Disarmament. We all wanted it known that the Prime Minister of Finland wishes us well. And that we wish him well. He is doing a good thing for disarmament. But there were very large numbers of distinguished representatives and visitors, and hearing a fraction of those we wanted to has taken a long time. We have thought a lot about this experience and we think that maybe on the next occasion we could instead have a press conference which could be open to those delegates who wished to come but which also allowed the press to question all these distinguished people and would solve the problem of opening the convention, allowing us to begin with the clash of relevant debate.

We have had many suggestions about how to organise things better, and there will be many more. Indeed, I beg you to send those suggestions in to us. You can write either to John Lambert at the address on the leaflet on which you enrolled, or directly to the Russell Foundation. And I will promise to present your advice: not just your complaints, but also the ideas about what should be maintained and what should be developed. I promise to present all these points before the liaison committee, where they will be thoroughly discussed and acted upon. We also know that many new groups wish to join the liaison committee and we beg them, because the time is now short, to write to us, to write about any proposal they wish to have considered, and to join us at our meetings.

Now I must deal with some announcements. Firstly, I should say that the liaison committee which struggled to make this conference, has already begun work and invites your help to make the next conference, in Berlin. We plan to gather there in May 1983. There is also another important meeting which is being proposed by our friends in Athens. And there are a variety of other proposals for further conventions in Italy and elsewhere. The next convention in Berlin is a definite fact. It is scheduled. The people have begun to organise. It will take place in May in 1983 and we invite your active participation and your active involvement.

When I was last in Berlin it was Good Friday. We went, Michael Meacher and I, to see Robert Havemann. To our great distress he died just as we arrived. But we crossed over to see him and we saw other good friends in East Berlin and good friends in West Berlin also. We crossed back at the checkpoint where we saw the control posts, and the landscape of barbed wire, and we saw that bleak pathway which takes us back to the origins of our present predicament. And I thought then there could be no more suitable place to go to than Berlin for our next big formal session.

People have said to me "are you sure the peace movement is mature enough? Will this be a provocation? Could there be difficulties?". Yes, there will be difficulties. No, this will not be a provocation. The peace movement is a great force and a growing force. We can go to Berlin and we can take to that capital a message which tells all Europe what the peace movement really is. And this can only help us to develop the struggle that we are engaged in. When I stood in the middle of that wilderness between the two Berlins, suspended between two Europes, I was reminded of some words of the poet Auden which have often moved me. He wrote then, at the beginning of the Second World War, at the beginning of this conflict which tore us in halves, a profoundly pacifist

utterance which concluded with just one line, which is this:
"We must love one another or die."

It is in that spirit, dear friends, that we shall meet again in Berlin and that we shall work together between now and then to make certain that our next conference is a fitting development of this one.

(ii) Enlarging the Dialogue

Speech given at the opening session of the Berlin Convention on European Nuclear Disarmament in May 1983.

This Second European Nuclear Disarmament Convention arrives in Berlin at a time when the peace movement faces a more awesome challenge than ever before. When we launched the Appeal for European Nuclear Disarmament in April 1980, we warned that "we are entering the most dangerous decade in human history". The dangers are already abundantly apparent. The deployment of new nuclear weapons in Europe continues, and although the campaign against all such weapons has gained overwhelming public support in many countries, further military escalation is everywhere in prospect. We should heed the warning of Alva Myrdal that the nuclear gaming of the superpowers has embroiled Europe into blocs which were not of its own making, has created preparations for a war which advances no European interest, and has deployed both weapons and doctrines which, unless opposed, will bring about the sacrifice of the European peoples and their civilisation. Nuclear gaming takes place in the calculated placement of the silos and the transporters which harbour the engines of destruction; but it also takes place across conference tables from which all European victims are excluded. As we watch the proposals and counter-proposals in arms control negotiations, we are bound to note that their open logic is accompanied by an unstated but dreadful logic of implication. Arguments about military balance go to and fro. But as the balance tilts, so the threats become less controlled. If Pershing II missiles are brought to Germany, then the Soviet Union may have to adopt a policy of "launch on warning". The argument is remorseless. If a missile can arrive from the West to the East in six minutes or less, then there is no time for sophisticated checks on the intentions who sent it. Or of those who

may not have sent it. In a recent 18 months period which was monitored by researchers there were 147 false alerts, each of which could have been terminal for our continent had launch on warning been the actual instruction in force in Soviet Command Headquarters.

For this reason the peace movements have to pay attention to the arms control negotiations. We have to insist that the recent positive proposals put forward by Mr Andropov should be carefully examined, and constructively met by NATO. Day-to-day our survival is under menace and no-one can afford to ignore the fateful arguments which are in progress at Geneva.

But no-one can afford to rest their hopes on the outcome of such talks alone. In each country, the peace movements develop their own policies, and many already insist upon action which is direct and simple. In Britain, an overwhelming majority of our people do not want to participate in this new round of the arms race. We have decided to refuse the new missiles, and our refusal is unconditional. We wish to remove all nuclear bases from our territory, and to embark upon a non-nuclear defence policy. At the same time, the realisation has dawned among us that we are part of the mainland, and that our security depends upon the peace of Europe in a nuclear-free zone covering the entire territory between the superpowers. And even this we see as but a beginning in the struggle to banish nuclear weapons from the relationship between the States throughout the world.

All these things are certainly a matter of action, but they also need much discussion, and international exchanges. This is the burden of Alva Myrdal's special message to this Convention, which is the third she has sent us. As you will see, she speaks of our need to prepare ourselves for a new phase. To do this, we must draw closer, and discuss more.

This Convention meets as part of the pluriform culture of Europe, and the incredible diversity of its political structures. Our goal of continental nuclear disarmament is shared by all of us. But the approach to it must perforce vary from one country to the next, within the different political and military conditions which apply. That is why we have chosen a conference of workshops, encouraging meetings between people with similar problems, representatives of similar interests, possibilities of primary co-operation. In our workshops, trade unionists may agree on whatever joint approaches are practicable for them; women's groups may come together to co-ordinate their actions in ways

◀ *At the end of the Berlin Convention, 1983.*

which they find appropriate; churches will establish the terms of their own dialogue and continued association. There is no central committee hanging over this process of direct communication, no body of "wise men" who can manipulate our convergence, which will either be free and generously spontaneous, or null and void. It is for this reason that our plenary meetings are not central to our activity in the way that many conferences of political parties or trade unions have established their central fora. Ours is a movement to bring together ordinary people from many different countries and many levels of influence and activity. Our work will result not in proclamations, but in joint agreement and common activities.

There are so many things which divide us. These divisions cannot be hidden and no-one will benefit from trying to conceal them. We are examining a complex issue in a complex continent. All of us are perfectly aware that the de-nuclearisation of our continent would be our de-alignment from the blocs. Most of us seek to approach such de-alignment by careful steps, gingerly, noting that there is a delicate balance between the ponderous structures from whose deathly shadow we wish to escape. We need to establish the autonomous choice of our peoples, and to build new relationships which rest on trust and co-operation. But all new relationships must threaten old ones. That is one of the reasons why the Appeal for European Nuclear Disarmament aroused fears, often irrational fears, on both sides of Europe's divide. There are numerous important people in the West who insist that we are working for the Russians, while at least one prominent Soviet spokesman alleges that we are employed by NATO. This is one area in which the truth is less complicated than it seems to such commentators. Neither side employs us, although we would be very happy if both would send their contributions to meet our conference deficit. It is in the constructive nature of our work that our critics will find their response, and there can be no doubt this will be a convincing one.

More and more of us have come to see the wars which are seeded throughout the world as threatening our own security, and of posing dangers which could spill back into Europe from other zones.

In Brussels, because the conflict in the Middle East was so directly related to our concerns, we agreed to make contact with the Israeli Peace Movement. It must be said that the war in the Lebanon subsequently became more brutal, and that the predicament of the Palestinian people is still becoming daily more unbearable. There remains a vivid danger that the superpowers could come to blows as a result of that conflict. If they did, the cruise missile base in Comiso could be the inlet through which nuclear war roared into Europe.

The wars in Central America have escalated to displace from people's minds the nasty little battle of the Falkland Islands about which we Britons spoke with such a sense of shame during our Brussels meeting. I hope we will be hearing from those peace movements who have been exploring contact in Nicaragua and elsewhere in Latin America. A bloody conflict rages in Afghanistan, and this renders more difficult the Sino-Soviet detente which is just as necessary to the peace of Europe as that of Western detente for which we must all work.

The world is one world. If SS20 missiles were, as a result of arms control negotiations, to be moved from the European frontier into Soviet Asia, the threat would have been exported from Europe to China, and the result would be still further tension and peril. I am not suggesting that Europeans can negotiate for Chinese or *vice versa:* but it seems clear that a priority task of the European peace movements must be to link hands, not only with those who seek peace in the Soviet Union and Eastern Europe, but also with people from China, and all those nations in the Third and Fourth Worlds which verge upon starvation whilst they are nudged towards Armageddon.

Workshops in the conference will explore some of these issues. They will also explore the problems of dialogue between different political and social structures. Such dialogue is difficult to arrange. Our own invitations to the Soviet and East European Peace Committees were sometimes declined, because some people objected to the wording of the Appeal for European Nuclear Disarmament, which has been the basic platform of these Conventions since they first began to shape up at the consultation in Rome in 1981. We very much regret that our invitations to dialogue were not accepted. We should still like to find appropriate ways in which the discussion of common interests, and common problems could begin. We are actively exploring the various proposals for new initiatives, which we hope may succeed where our previous efforts have failed. We must certainly organise extensive discussion within the Liaison Committee about these issues.

Some private citizens from Eastern Europe and Turkey who wished to join us have not been permitted to do so. They have empty chairs in the auditorium which are marked here, because it is necessary for us to protest when people are hindered in the effort to talk about peace.

The group for Building Confidence and Trust in Moscow wished to be with us but could not get exit permits. They have sent a paper by Mr Batovrin, which is being circulated.

The Hungarian Peace Group for Dialogue wished to send nine persons, but did not get exit permits. If their papers arrive we shall circulate them. Other Hungarian citizens, including Mihaly Vajda and Miklos Harasti asked to come and have sent us their greetings.

Forty-two people from the German Democratic Republic told us they were asking for exit permits, but they have not yet received them. Twenty-two of these people have sent us a message which will be made available as soon as possible.

Five people from Charter 77 said they wished to come, but they have not yet received passports. Mr Palous, Charter spokesman, sent a message to the Convention which will be distributed. Jiri Dienstbier has also sent a letter for distribution. From the Charter itself we received a message signed by five people including Jiri Hayek. Vaculik sent a letter signing our Appeal.

Our invitation to fellow Europeans was based upon a commitment of open access, and it was and remains our intention that all who wish to participate should be free to do so. There are so many people in Europe for whom disarmament is a burning priority that the discussion across frontiers will be hindered by denial of passports but it cannot be stopped.

As one of our Dutch friends has put it, we need a trilateral dialogue: between Western peace people and private citizens in Eastern Europe, but also between Western peace movements and the official representatives of the East European countries.

Disarmament is a complicated question nowadays, and the approach to it is even more complicated.

Let me give an example. Very many of us have been involved in protests to the Turkish Government about the suppression of the Turkish Peace Movement. In Brussels, Mr Dikerdem made a poignant statement about the treatment meted out to the President of that movement, his father. No-one will expect that we should apologise for joining our voices to his. At the same time, our Romanian friends have informed us that the same Turkish Government which is persecuting our friends has made a very positive reply to the UN Secretary General's inquiry concerning the establishment of nuclear-weapon-free zones. Of course this reply will be welcomed to the extent that it helps in the process of de-nuclearising the Balkan area. We must ask our workshop on this question to evaluate these Turkish Government proposals, and to seek also the advice of our Greek friends on their meaning. We are sure that this will be done with open minds. I believe it is not unreasonable to suggest that what must obviously apply in the case of the repressive Government of Turkey can also apply in our relations with other States which maintain widely different styles of Government.

Our insistence that we should be able to talk about peace freely with all Europeans, everywhere, is simply an elementary rule of procedure. But our desire to bring forward areas of agreement for disarmament is a fundamental objective to which we are all committed. Those who see contradictions here must realise that the contradictions are not in our commitment, but in the shape of a world which we are struggling to change.

Bertrand Russell told a story about how he once got lost in the country and asked a local person the way to Bristol. "Bristol", the man said, "if I was going there, I wouldn't start from here".

But we do start here, in this most difficult world. *We have got to get agreement.*

That is why, while we carry forward this discussion among ourselves, we must also continue to seek, by every reasonable means, to enlarge our scope for dialogue. We would certainly value help from anyone who could help us to find the way to solve this problem for our next big meeting.

Now, there is work to do. I thank you all for your kind attention, and look forward to the real exchanges in our workshops.

The Italian END Convention, 1984.

HERESIES
Resist Much, Obey Little
Ken Coates

Writing in *Tribune*, **PERRY ANDERSON said:**

"The collection of essays brought together in *Heresies* has its common focus in the fate of communism in Europe, East and West. Ken Coates ranges over a wide spectrum of figures and subjects — from Stalin, Trotsky and Bukharin to Tito or Pollitt, from Lysenko to Sakharov, from Berlinguer to Cornforth.

Two qualities of writing stand out immediately and memorably — each equally rare. The first is the historical breadth of vision, and warmth of imaginative sympathy, that Coates brings to bear on the experience of the international communist movement, from an independent socialist standpoint outside it.

As a long-time militant on the other side of the great divide separating the European Labour movement since the twenties, he has a stronger and more spontaneous sense of its underlying unities than perhaps any other recent analyst of the British Left. G.D.H. Cole — an honourable contender — seems dry and remote by comparison.

As Coates puts it: "A lot of words and a lot of blood have combined over the years to separate socialist and communist traditions in Europe. Yet there remains an uneasy sense of common origins, and perhaps a hesitant fraternity, not completely forgotten even while all the horrors of a dreadful century are strongly remembered".

The second hallmark of Coates's writings is its tone. Formally, many of the pieces in *Heresies* were composed as book reviews — most of them for *Tribune*, to which he expresses his loyalty and gratitude. But actually, most of them dwell rather little on the detailed contents of the volumes that are their occasion.

What they really represent is a series of interventions, both thoughtful and passionate, in contemporary debates on the Left — crisp, clear and free-standing *commentary* on people, ideas and events, of great moral and political urgency.

To read *Heresies* is to realise how unusual this kind of writing is on the Left, as a consistent practice, and how valuable. We have many self-declared theoreticians, and nearly as many rhetoricians, in the ranks of British socialism today. But practical, critical, responsible engagement with the major international issues of the time, on a regular basis — of that we have very little. At his best, there is no one who can write so well in this mode as Coates.

The two outstanding examples of this gift in the present volume, to my mind, are the essays on Solzhenitsyn and on Kolakowski. Coates's assessment of Solzhenitsyn, deeply felt and beautifully written, is the most acute and balanced reflection on the novelist, and his historical significance, that I have yet seen. It ends with the following comment on Solzhenitsyn's famous *Letter to the Soviet Leaders:*

"We need to face the last great enigma posed by this puzzling man: which is not how he could personally develop such strange opinions, but how the social occasion in which they flourish could survive. The opinions themselves are obviously no remedy for the ills of Soviet society, but they *are* part of its disease, and will likely persist until this is understood".

The deflation of Kolakowski's rhodomontades against Marxism is done in a very different tone, with a light, deft irony that still concludes with a vital general point:

"All the good people who won't ever hear about this book, or about any of the books it concerns, because they are toiling in mills and factories, mines and offices, will still need to keep a small anchor on the utopias Kolakowski rejects, if any atom of their social power is to be usable to retain for us any of that wide range of limited freedoms which he wishes to uphold . . . You can begin to defend people against little injustices if there is a larger justice around, be it only at the back of your own mind".

If there is sometimes quickness of temper in Coates's responses, it is a small price to pay for the basic decency and generosity of his outlook. So even when an author gets less than full justice (one thinks of Balibar, now a fellow-militant in END), the result is still a pungent statement in its own right on the issue of socialist democracy, one of the principal themes of the book.

There are omissions one regrets. Asian communism is absent from the volume, although Coates has been deeply concerned with China and Indochina over the years, and his own work on Bukharin has recently been translated in Pekin. It would have been good to see his thoughts on Mao or Deng, Ho or Pol Pot, here too.

But there is a certain logic to his selection. *Heresies* is essentially about the past and future of the *European* Labour movement. It ends, appropriately enough, with articles whose summons to action against the nuclear arms race foreshadowed the birth of END, of whose conception Coates seems from this evidence to have been the original initiator.

In that perspective, one looks forward to a companion volume on the Social-Democratic heritage, and prospects, in Europe — with pieces on, say, the Palme-Kreisky-Brandt discussions, Mitterrand's ineffable diaries, the values of the novels of Böll and Grass, the memoirs of Mario Soares, not to speak of our own Michael Foot's homages to Disraeli, Beaverbrook and co.

A heretical vision of this sharpness must necessarily be a two-eyed one. Meanwhile, this handsomely produced volume — some of the accompanying photographs are semi-archival items — is good news enough".

Paper £3.50   *ISBN 0 85124 356 8*
Cloth £13.95   *ISBN 0 85124 355 X*
158 pages with 14 illustrations

Spokesman, Bertrand Russell House, Gamble Street, Nottingham
Tel. 0602 708318